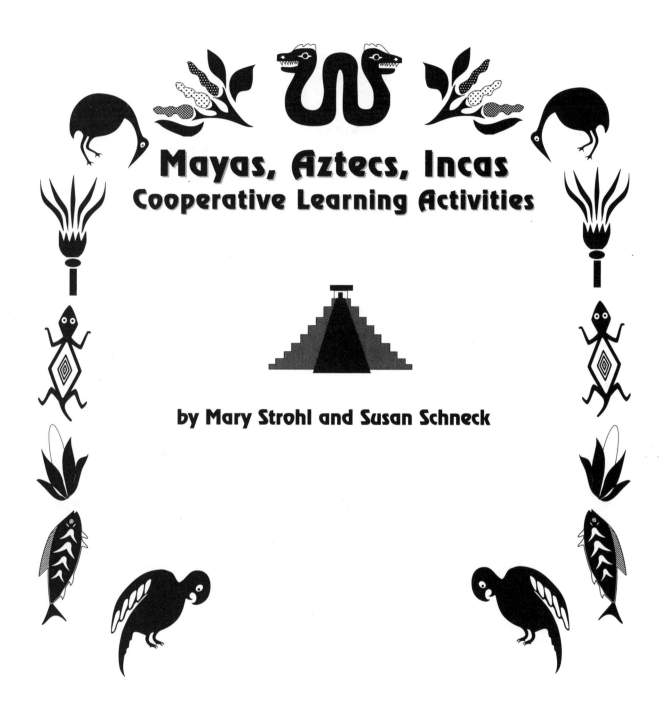

Mayas, Aztecs, Incas
Cooperative Learning Activities

by Mary Strohl and Susan Schneck

SCHOLASTIC
PROFESSIONAL BOOKS

New York • Toronto • London • Auckland • Sydney

About the Authors

Susan Schneck and Mary Strohl have many years combined experience in education and publishing. In 1986 they formed their own studio, Flights of Fancy, specializing in children's activity products and elementary teaching materials. In 1991 Mary moved to Durham, North Carolina, with her husband, Harlan. Sue remains in Racine, Wisconsin with her husband, Bob, and their two daughters Kate and Jenny. Mary and Sue continue their creative alliance via phone, FAX, and "working vacations." This is their sixth title for Scholastic Professional Books.

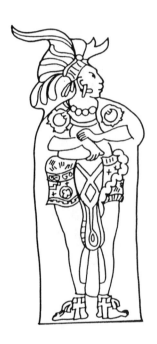

Special Thanks to

RT Computer Graphics
for their permission to use designs from:

The Santa Fe Collection
Native American & Southwest Clip Art

Cover design by Susan Schneck and Vincent Ceci
Illustrations by Susan Schneck

ISBN 0-590-49504-6
Copyright © 1994 by Flights of Fancy. All rights reserved.

Printed in the U.S.A.

Table of Contents

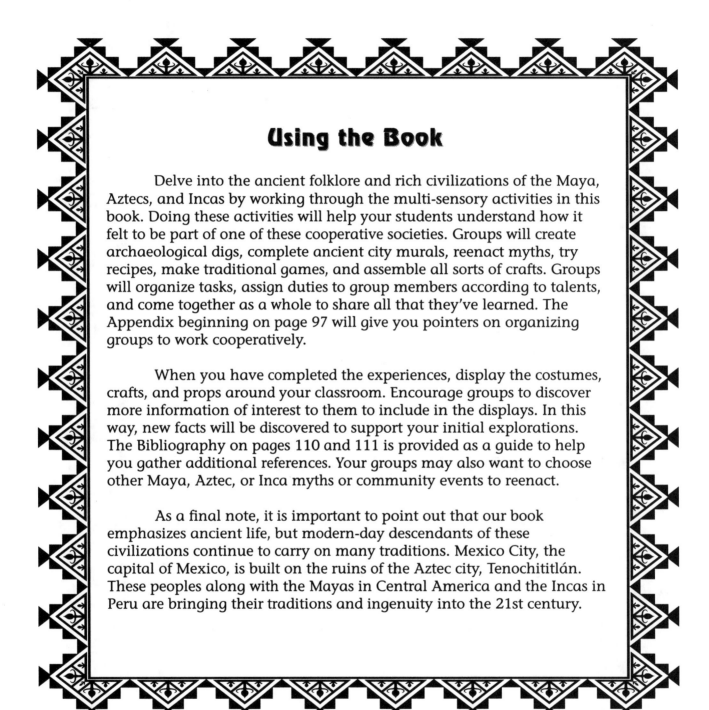

Using the Book

Delve into the ancient folklore and rich civilizations of the Maya, Aztecs, and Incas by working through the multi-sensory activities in this book. Doing these activities will help your students understand how it felt to be part of one of these cooperative societies. Groups will create archaeological digs, complete ancient city murals, reenact myths, try recipes, make traditional games, and assemble all sorts of crafts. Groups will organize tasks, assign duties to group members according to talents, and come together as a whole to share all that they've learned. The Appendix beginning on page 97 will give you pointers on organizing groups to work cooperatively.

When you have completed the experiences, display the costumes, crafts, and props around your classroom. Encourage groups to discover more information of interest to them to include in the displays. In this way, new facts will be discovered to support your initial explorations. The Bibliography on pages 110 and 111 is provided as a guide to help you gather additional references. Your groups may also want to choose other Maya, Aztec, or Inca myths or community events to reenact.

As a final note, it is important to point out that our book emphasizes ancient life, but modern-day descendants of these civilizations continue to carry on many traditions. Mexico City, the capital of Mexico, is built on the ruins of the Aztec city, Tenochititlán. These peoples along with the Mayas in Central America and the Incas in Peru are bringing their traditions and ingenuity into the 21st century.

About the Ancient Peoples

The study of these ancient civilizations is a celebration of the talents and traditions of their peoples. The Maya, Aztecs, and Incas designed and built massive temples, beautiful stone palaces, and busy cities complete with water and sewer systems. Some of the roads they used as trade routes are still in use today. Their legacies also include contributions to science and astronomy. We also can learn from their mistakes. Some scholars believe that the Maya abandoned their cities because of overpopulation, war, and misuse of the environment.

Highly spiritual peoples, the Maya, Aztecs, and Incas placed little distinction between the everyday rules of society and the strict order of conduct required by the gods that ruled their worlds. According to their religions, gods assured when the sun rose, the rain fell, and determined whether crops were plentiful. Human sacrifice, though thought cruel by "our standards," was often viewed as a sacred act that honored victims and pleased gods.

Maya, Aztec, and Inca leaders had absolute power over all society. They were warriors, fighting for control of other cities. But, many leaders also served the needs of the people, seeing that they were well-fed and housed. Each individual had specific personal and civic responsibilities, be it as farmers, priests, soldiers, merchants, rulers, or craftspeople. Each community member paid tax in the form of service.

The Mayas had left their cities and faded from prominence by 1480. Their cities were soon lost to the overgrowth of the rain forest. Once Europeans arrived in the Americas, they conquered the people they encountered and destroyed much of their civilizations. Hernan Cortez conquered the Aztecs in 1521; Pizarro overthrew the Incas in 1532. Today archaeologists continue to discover more about each of these ancient civilizations. It is an ongoing process that will bring new insights to all of us for years to come.

Reference Maps and Dates

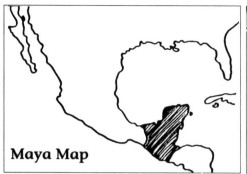

Maya Map

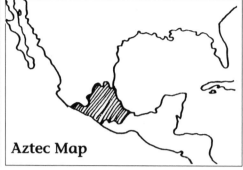

Aztec Map

Inca Map

Maya Dates

3114 BC: Beginning of the Maya calendar.

250-625 AD: Classic Period when farming communities establish on the Yucatan Peninsula. Many Maya cities built.

625-800: Cultural development of writing, sculpture, pottery, architecture.

800-950: Period of collapse. Many cities are abandoned. People farm land outside the cities.

1190: Chichén Itzá falls. The Maya flourish on the Yucatan Peninsula (up until 1450).

1460: Hurricane hits the peninsula.

1470: Plague prevalent.

1500: Spanish begin conquest of Maya.

1500-Present: Many Maya still live in Mexico, keeping many of their customs and rituals.

Aztec Dates

900 AD: Warlike Toltecs establish an empire in the Valley of Mexico.

1000: Aztecs enter the Valley of Mexico where little farmland is left to settle.

1300-1400: The Aztecs build their capital city of Tenochititlán on an island in Lake Texcoco. They were continually at war and conquered the Valley of Mexico and some neighboring lands.

1440-1470: Montezuma I is king. Parts of the island are reclaimed. Aztec empire expands into the south and the Gulf Coast.

1500-1520: Height of the Aztec Empire. Montezuma II is king.

1520: Hernán Cortés and Spanish army conquer Tenochititlán. After slavery and disease, almost no trace of the Aztec Empire remains.

Inca Dates

400 AD: Incas settle in farming communities in the Andes Mountains and valleys of present-day Peru.

1100-1200: Cuzco settled and eventually becomes the capital of the Inca Empire.

1400-1500: Incas conquer lands to the north and south. The empire grows until the sixteenth century.

1532: Pizarro arrives in Peru. The Inca Empire is destroyed.

Present Day: Descendants of the Incas, who still speak the Inca language, live in poor settlements in the Andes Mountains. They still pray to their traditional gods.

Note: Shaded sections on maps indicate where these ancient civilizations settled.

Chapter 1

Ancient Cultures

Inca ruins at Machu Picchu

Background Information for the Teacher

The Maya, Aztecs, and Incas developed some of the greatest civilizations of the world. These societies were far more advanced than other cultures of that time. Their artifacts help us realize that these peoples were highly educated and cultured. Scholars and archaeologists study pre-Columbian artifacts to learn how people lived and what they accomplished.

The **Maya** built many cities including Copán, Tikal, Tulum, and Piedras Negras. Once scholars thought that only priests and officials lived in cities, but from excavations, they now know huge areas were covered with family compounds, farmlands, and roads to connect them.

The **Aztecs** were wanderers until they built their capital city of Tenochtitlán. Eventually through war and trade, they came to rule 5 million people from north of Tenochtitlán to present day Guatemala. The Aztecs were fine craftspeople making the implements they needed for their everyday and ritual lives.

The **Inca** empire at its peak had over 8 million inhabitants. Excellent stonemasons, the people had no need for mortar to hold their city walls and buildings intact. Inca bronzesmiths produced a variety of tools from tweezers to ceremonial objects. Inca agriculture was more advanced than the Maya or Aztecs. They terraced the land to conserve soil and water and used fertilizers to grow more crops.

In this chapter your class will create archaelogical digs for all three cultures, cooperatively draw murals of ancient cities, and create standing figures for each of the three societies. Students, too, will discover their own reasons to want to know more about the Maya, Aztec, and Inca empires.

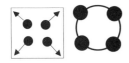

Social Skills: Participate, form groups quietly, work toward a goal.
Academic Skills: Use scientific methods of discovery to recreate an archaeological dig.
Teacher: Using the Task Card directions, your students will cooperatively create and methodically explore what it might be like to discover artifacts in a real archaeological dig. Note: Younger groups should work with fewer Co-Op Cards.

Archaeological Digs

ORGANIZING FOR THE DIGS
- Start with the Inca dig to get students accustomed to how a dig is organized.
- Set up stations around the classroom. Label them with the task names shown underlined below.
- Reproduce Task Cards (pages 10-11) for each group and gather materials required for each part of the dig.
- Prepare dig sites according to the size of your class. We recommend two dig sites for classes with 18 or more students.
- Ask students to go to stations that interest them or assign students to different stations.

STATIONS AND MATERIALS
1. <u>DIG EXPERT</u> sets up the dig.
   Materials: Task Cards; Co-Op Cards (divide between dig sites)
2. <u>ARTIFACT SPECIALIST</u> gathers artifacts.
   Materials: Task Cards; large, heavy, wax-lined bakery cake boxes (1–2 sheet); sandbox sand (to fill 2–3 inches of box); "artifacts" (from students' homes); ruler; marker; masking tape; scissors; string
3. <u>DIG SITE MANAGER</u> buries artifacts.
   Materials: Task Cards; spoons; plants, stones and other natural materials to landscape top of dig
4. <u>EXCAVATOR</u> excavates the dig site.
   Materials: Task Cards; small toothpicks; spoons; small, stiff paintbrushes
5. <u>DIG SECRETARY</u> describes the discoveries.
   Materials: Task Cards; data sheets; ruler; pen or pencil; colored pencils
6. <u>ARCHAEOLOGIST</u> identifies the artifacts.
   Materials: Task Cards; Co-Op Cards; pen or pencil

EXTENSION ACTIVITIES
- **Extension Activity 1:** MAYA, AZTEC DIGS: Use the Co-Op Cards on pages 13 and 14 in this section to create dig sites featuring other ancient cultures.
- **Extension Activity 2:** GUEST ARCHAEOLOGIST: If possible, ask a museum curator or archaeologist to bring in actual artifacts and describe the procedures used at a "real" dig.
- **Extension Activity 3:** BACK TO THE FUTURE-DIG: Imagine what it would be like for future cultures to uproot 20th century artifacts! Instead of the Co-Op Cards included, students cut out pictures from magazines of items from our present century/culture showing toys, homes, clothing, etc. Artifact Specialists will find lots of items from home, yard, and basements to use for artifacts.

Task Cards and Instructions

DIG EXPERT TASK CARD

Prepare one or two boxes depending on how many group members there are.

1. Place the box on a sturdy surface and fill it with 2–3" of sand.

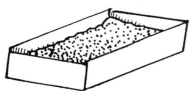

2. Prepare the box for excavation by drawing lines along the sides, about 5" apart. Number the spaces along one side, and letter them alongside the other.

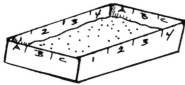

3. Place strings along these lines. This will form the "grid" which students will refer to when describing each artifact and where it was found.

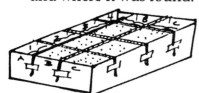

4. Get the **ARTIFACT SPECIALIST** when you're done.

ARTIFACT SPECIALIST TASK CARD

Divide the Co-Op Cards evenly among the groups of students.

1. Collect or make one artifact for one or two Co-Op Cards. If possible, use "real" materials from home or yard to make the items.
2. Think of ways to add details or "age" the artifact so that it looks really authentic.
3. Keep the artifacts that you have gathered a secret!

Co-op Card:

_____

Artifact Created:

4. Get the **DIG-SITE MANAGER** when you're done.

DIG-SITE MANAGER TASK CARD

Get artifacts from the ARTIFACT SPECIALIST. Gather tools and go to the dig site to do your work.

1. When all the artifacts have been gathered, "bury" them under the sand in different areas of the box, at different depths. Note: Some can be sticking up a bit, or mounded over with sand to make them look more authentic.
2. Bits of plants can also be added to the surface of the sand.
3. You might want to add stones to the surface to make it look authentic.
4. Keep a whisk broom and dustpan handy to sweep up any spills!

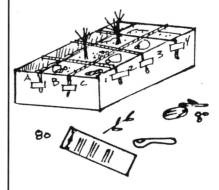

5. Get the **EXCAVATOR** when you're done.

Task Cards and Instructions

EXCAVATOR TASK CARD

Pick up tools from the DIG SITE MANAGER. Go to the dig site to do your work.

1. You will need "tools": toothpicks, spoons, and small brushes.
2. Each Excavator chooses a grid area to "dig" in. Gently, layer by layer, find the artifact.
3. Excavators can move to another grid area, but must not disturb other diggers. The object is to disturb the smallest amount of sand necessary to uncover the artifact. DO NOT REMOVE ARTIFACT FROM THE SAND!
4. Get the DIG SECRETARY to record your findings.

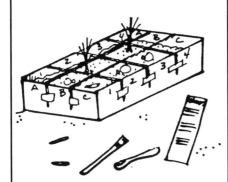

DIG SECRETARY TASK CARD

Pick up tools from the EXCAVATOR. Go to the dig site to do your work. Record your findings.

1. Who uncovered the artifact?_____

_____

2. Where was it found?
   grid letter:_____
   number:_____
3. How deep in the sand is the artifact?
   inches: _____
   metric: _____
4. Describe the area where the artifact was found. (Use the back of this card.)
5. Draw a sketch of the artifact below.

6. Give sketch to the ARCHAELOGIST.

ARCHAEOLOGIST TASK CARD

Using the DIG SECRETARY'S Task Card, try matching artifact to a Co-Op Card.

1. Explain to others in the group why you think the card and the artifact match.
2. At this point, the ARTIFACT SPECIALISTS tell if they think the ARCHAELOGIST has made a correct match.
3. Note: Even if an artifact and Co-Op Card do not match with the SPECIALIST'S, a group member who gives convincing evidence should get credit for being right!

Inca Dig Co-Op Cards

Cut cards apart and use with the Archaeological Dig activities on pages 9–11.

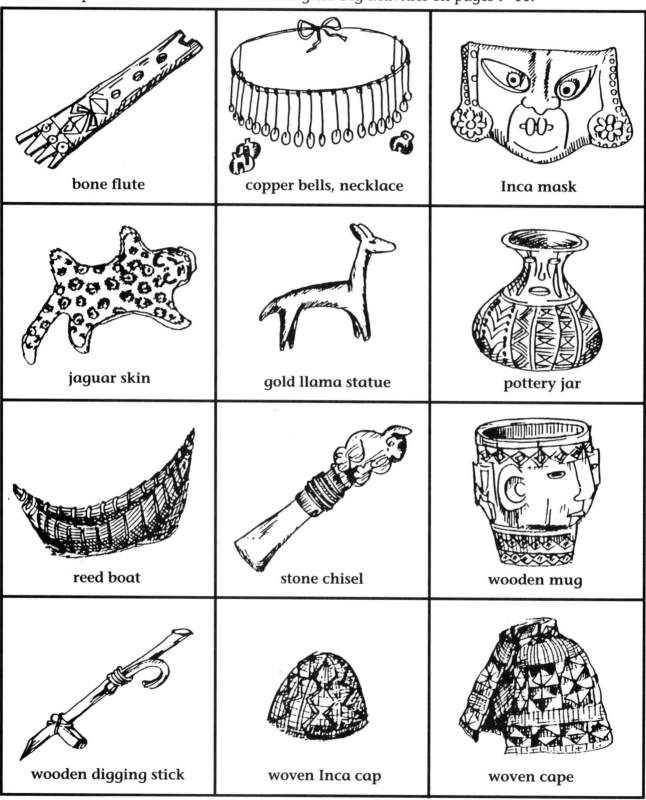

bone flute	copper bells, necklace	Inca mask
jaguar skin	gold llama statue	pottery jar
reed boat	stone chisel	wooden mug
wooden digging stick	woven Inca cap	woven cape

Maya Dig Co-Op Cards

Cut cards apart and use with the Archaeological Dig activities on pages 9–11.

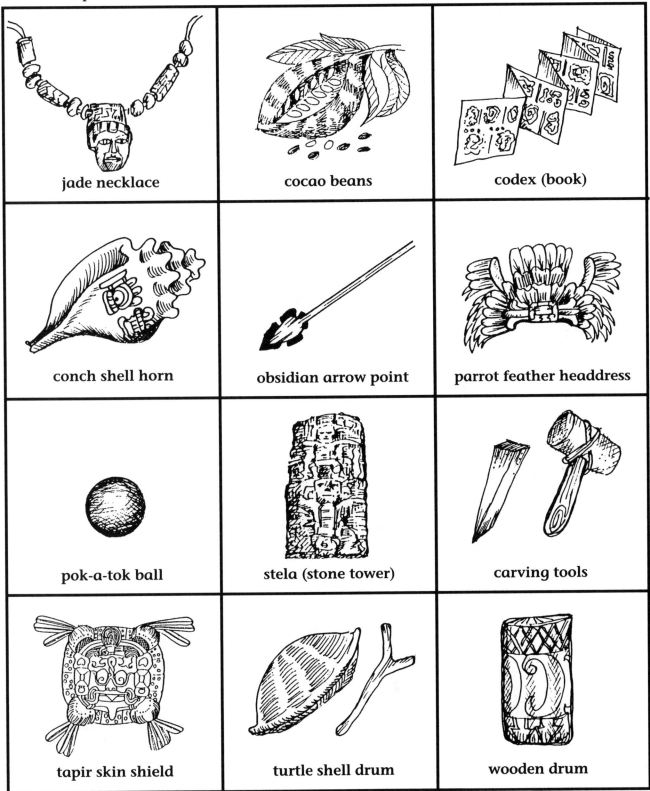

jade necklace	cocao beans	codex (book)
conch shell horn	obsidian arrow point	parrot feather headdress
pok-a-tok ball	stela (stone tower)	carving tools
tapir skin shield	turtle shell drum	wooden drum

Aztec Dig Co-Op Cards

Cut cards apart and use with the Archaeological Dig activities on pages 9–11.

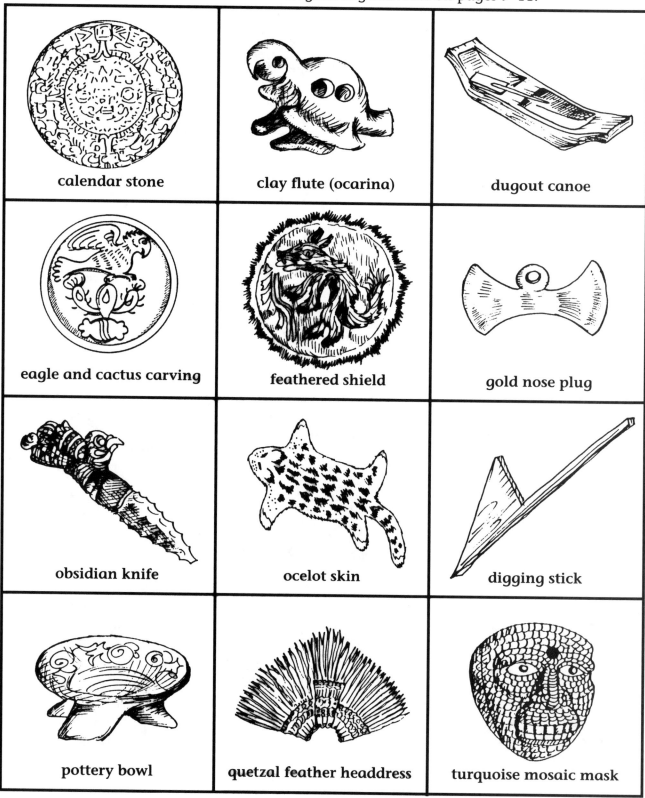

calendar stone	clay flute (ocarina)	dugout canoe
eagle and cactus carving	feathered shield	gold nose plug
obsidian knife	ocelot skin	digging stick
pottery bowl	quetzal feather headdress	turquoise mosaic mask

Social Skills: Seek accuracy, integrate ideas into a whole, and work together toward a goal.
Academic Skills: Use mapping skills to create a cooperative large-scale mural of an ancient city.
Teacher: This activity will help your students develop accurate work habits and team skills. Encourage your students to work in pencil as they map out their sections, making sure all their pieces match. Repeat this activity. Your students will enjoy the challenge and get better at drawing to scale!

Group Organization for Co-Op Draw-a-City Scenes

ORGANIZING THE CITY SCENES

- This is a drawing activity where students redraw one small section of a scene onto larger paper to make a cooperative display. By working in groups, students do sections of four to put together into a larger scene (approximately 27" x 33"). Students might want to divide the sections in quarters, strips, or bands (see below). Note: Instructions in Extension Activities show you how to make even larger murals.
- It is recommended that each scene be completed by 16 children (4 groups of 4). You can work with half of your class at a time with each group completing a different scene.
- Start by reproducing a copy of one of the scenes: Maya (page 17), Inca (page 19), Aztec (page 21).
- Make a "master plan" for each student group. Divide the reproducible scene using heavy marker in one of three ways shown below.

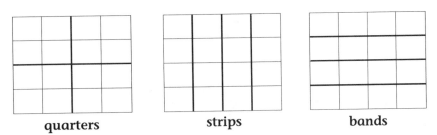

quarters   strips   bands

- Complete the grid by planning which section each group will draw. Then write each group member's name in each grid space.
- Make two copies of the master grid. Cut one grid into the 4-part sections for each group to refer to as they work. Cut the other into single-grid sections for each child to draw from.
- Gather the additional materials listed below for each group.

MATERIALS

- scene grid sections (as described above)
- drawing paper (6 3/4" x 8 1/4" for a 27" x 33" mural)
- pencils, erasers, markers or crayons
- heavy-duty masking tape (for assembling the mural panels)
- cord in three different colors (for attaching fact captions to illustrations)

COMPLETING THE CITY SECTIONS (for each group member)
1. Ask students to use a pencil to reproduce elements from the small drawing onto the larger drawing sheet. Ask students to check these things:
   - Is your drawing right side up? Which side is longer, shorter?
   - How many lines meet the edge of the paper? Are they in the upper, middle or bottom part? Which sides are they on? Right, left, top, bottom?
   - Which of the lines on your section run off to another section? Whose section "connects" with yours? (Check with that group member to see how they "line up." Erase and redraw as needed on both sections.)
   - Have you drawn all the lines and artwork in your section? (Check against your larger drawing.)
2. When drawing is complete, ask groups to make sure their sketches align with those of corresponding groups.
3. Ask students to plan as a group what colors they'll be using. Then, have students color cooperatively.
4. When all the sections are done, tape them together along the back with masking tape.

ASSEMBLING THE CITY SECTIONS (for teacher or assigned group)
1. Refer to the master grid to find and position each group's section.
2. Place the four large sections face down in position on the floor.
3. Use wide masking tape to reinforce seams and edges of the sections.
4. Lift and view your cooperative masterpiece! Display on a bulletin board, wall, or hallway.

ADDING THE CITY FACTS (for each group)
1. Reproduce fact cards for each scene. Give two cards to each group.
2. Ask each group to find out two more facts about their scene. Have groups place all four facts along the outside of the mural.
3. Using colored cord or yarn, students can "match" the fact to the appropriate place on the scene. Note: Numbers in the small scenes on the fact pages correspond with the numbered facts.

EXTENSION ACTIVITIES
Extension Activity 1: ANCIENT CITY WALL FRIEZE: Increase the size of the drawing grid to 150% for one of the scenes to create a giant 54" x 66" mural. Students may need to take extra care to work accurately at this magnification.
Extension Activity 2: MAKE-A-PUZZLE: This is a good "get up and move" activity when you do not have time for drawing. Reproduce a scene onto an 11" x 17" sheet. Make two copies. Divide one copy into two-part sections to create a large-size master grid for classroom reference. Cut up the other copy and hand out the individual sections to all the students. Students "match" their piece with those around them by looking on the master chart. Later, partners look for others in their "row", above them, etc. The class completes the puzzle.

Maya Draw-a-City Scene

Talum was a thriving Mayan seaside city.

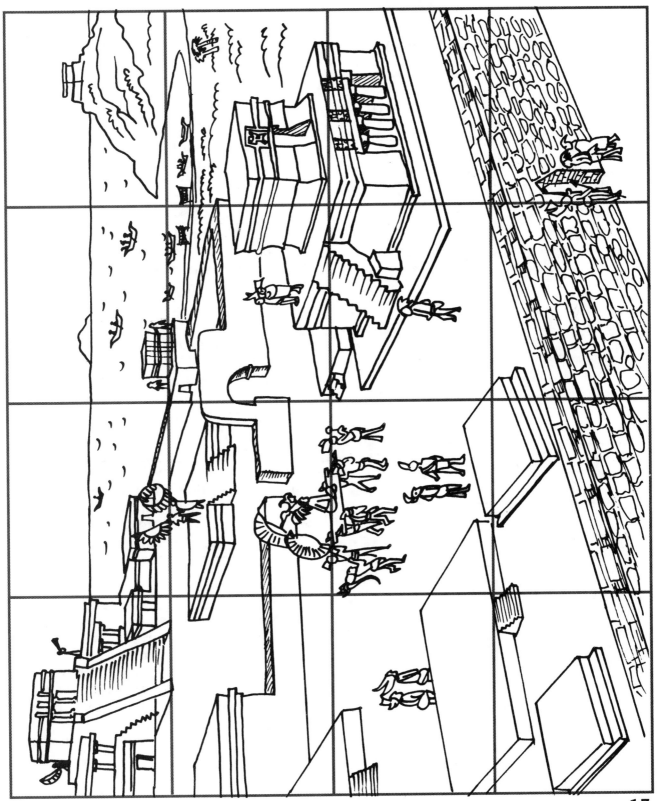

Maya Draw-a-City Facts

Cut facts apart and put them around your mural. String colored cord between fact cards and the areas the card describes. Research library books to get more facts about Mayan cities.

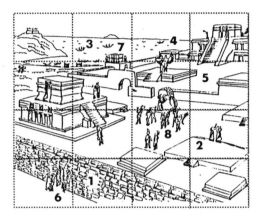

1. **Tulum**, a seaport city, had blue and white walls that were repainted each year.

2. **Stone platforms** were often used for plays. Actors wore masks to illustrate the parts they played. Plays often had religious ties.

3. The Maya fished and brought in trade goods in dug-out canoes. Some were 40' long, 4' wide with 12 oars per side.

4. The **temple** was surrounded by houses of priests and nobles. Few ordinary Mayas lived in Tulum, because there was little fresh water. They had *cenotes*, underground wells, to catch rainwater.

5. The center of the city was a large **plaza** where ceremonies, dances, and festivals were held.

6. When guards saw travelers approach city gates, they would play drums. Warriors would immediately stand on walls with spears in hand. If the travelers were friendly, the gates were opened.

7. Each town had a **traveler's house** with food, firewood, and water provided for out-of-town travelers.

8. A **procession** of the governor (Halach Uinic) was led by guards blowing conch shells. Following them were warriors carrying spears. Then two trumpeters walked before the governor, who was carried on a *litter*. The litter was a stretcher with a feather canopy and a wooden throne.

Inca Draw-a-City Scene

A royal journey from an Inca mountain village

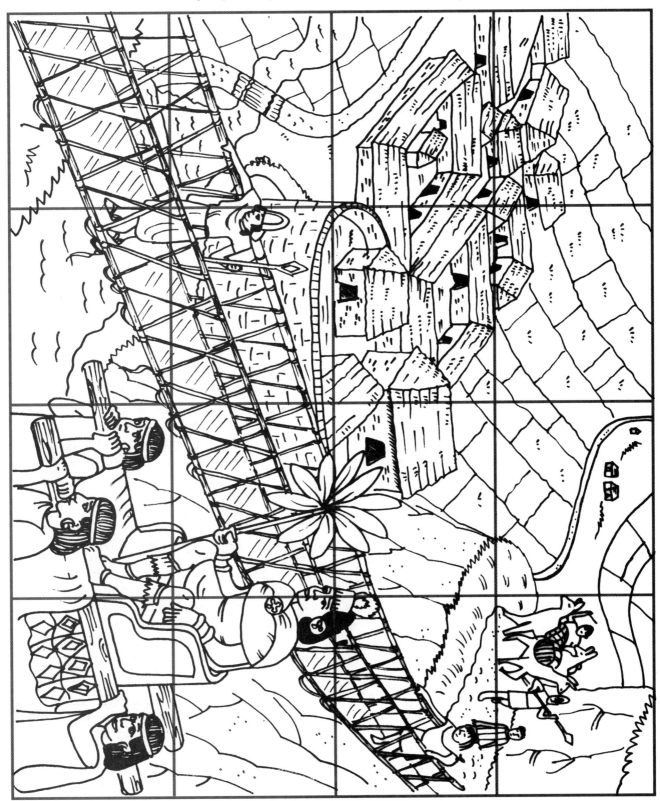

Inca Draw-a-City Facts

Cut facts apart and put them around your mural. String colored cord between fact card and the areas the card describes. Research library books to get more facts about Inca cities.

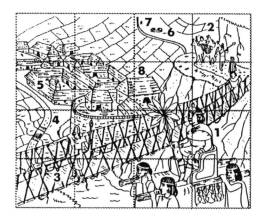

1. The **Emperor**, carried by servants on a royal *litter*, traveled along Inca roads. Litters were stretchers decorated with gems and gold and used for transporting royalty. Wheels were never used by the Incas.

2. Men on foot drove **llamas** which carried goods, not people. A "train" of a hundred llamas could only travel about 9 – 12 miles a day.

4. **Highways** made of cobbled stone were built throughout the Inca empire, along the coast and in the mountains. They linked every town and village. Each highway was named after the Emperor who built it.

3. **Suspension bridges**, built of heavy fiber ropes and twisted vines, made it possible for Incas to travel across deep valleys. People who lived near bridges were expected to keep them in working condition.

6. **Tambos** were rest houses that were spaced along roads at a day's journey apart. Some were for travelers' use; others, for government business.

5. **Villages** were made up of a number of compounds. Each walled compound contained several family's buildings and storehouses. Peasant houses were rectangular with thatched roofs.

7. Smaller shelters along the roads were used to house young men who served as messengers, delivering goods and mail to the next shelter.

8. Depending on the region, Inca homes were made of wood (hot damp eastern slopes), stone (cold mountain areas), or adobe bricks (warmer coasts).

Aztec Draw-a-City Scene

Tenochtitlán, Aztec capital

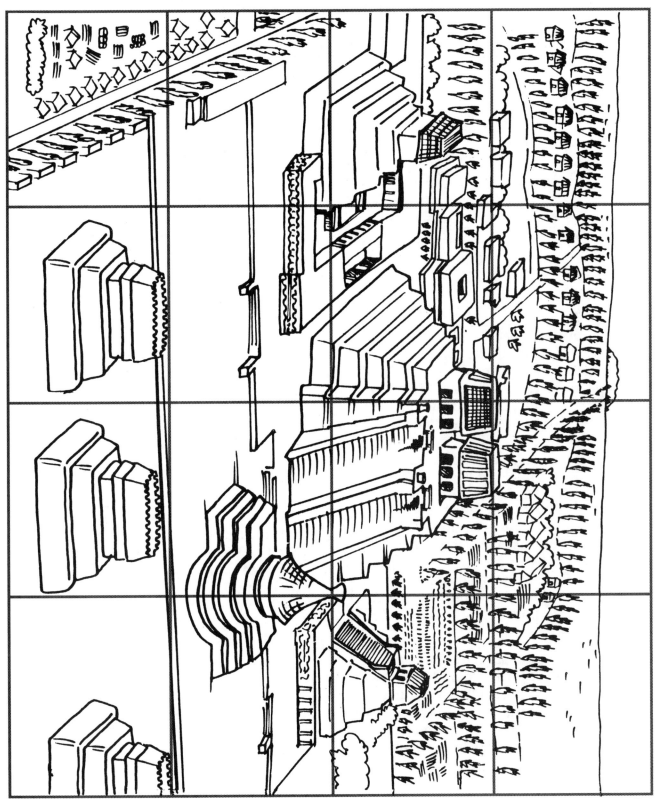

Aztec Draw-a-City Facts

Cut facts apart and put them around your mural. String colored cord between fact cards and the areas the card describes. Research library books to get more facts about Aztec cities.

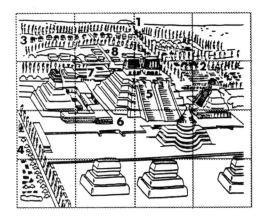

1. **Tenochtitlán** was built on the swampy lagoons in the center of lake Texcoco. *Causeways*, level bridges over the water from the mainland, had removable sections to protect the city from enemy armies.

2. Island gardens called "**chinampas**" on the outskirts of the city were used for growing food, flowers, and medicinal plants. Families grew food for themselves and for trade.

3. City **suburbs** ringed the outer edges of this city. Over half a million craftsmen and traders lived there. Each day, over 60,000 people traveled the *canals* of the city in dugout canoes. The canals furrowed the city and were used as aqueducts and thoroughfares.

6. The **Temple Precinct** included the temples houses for priests, their students, and the sacred ball court. Ball courts were used for ritual games played by the noblity. Some games were life and death matches.

4. **Markets** were held every five days throughout the city. People came to trade news, food, clothing, pottery, tobacco, pipes, and even slaves. There was no money used, instead Aztecs *bartered*, traded in cocoa beans, or paid in quills filled with gold dust for the goods they wanted. A jade necklace had the highest value.

7. The **Royal Palace**, home of the Emperor was the heart of the empire. The Emperor lived on the upper floor. On the first floor were the council hall, courts, arsenal, and treasury. The palace was so large that 4,000 could gather inside.

5. The magnificent **Great Temple of Tenochititlán** with gold and precious stones had secret chambers filled with offerings. At the top of the temple twin shrines honored *Tlaloc* (left), the god of rain and fertility, and *Huitzilopochtli* (the blue hummingbird), the god of sun and war.

8. **Houses of nobles** surrounded the royal palace. Though not as grand, they had more rooms, luxurious furnishings, and gardens that the common people did not have. Nobles included warrior chiefs and officials who helped the emperor rule.

Maya Civilization Stand-Ups

Color and cut out the people. Stand them near of the appropriate mural or use them to embellish dioramas, to create city scenes, or use with reports.

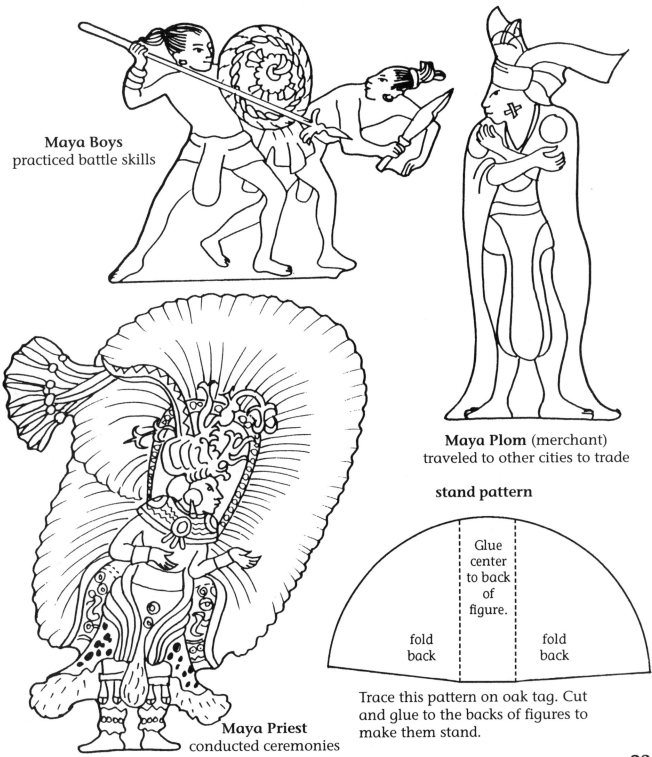

Maya Boys
practiced battle skills

Maya Plom (merchant)
traveled to other cities to trade

stand pattern

Glue center to back of figure.

fold back

fold back

Maya Priest
conducted ceremonies

Trace this pattern on oak tag. Cut and glue to the backs of figures to make them stand.

23

Maya Civilization Stand-Ups

(Use with stand pattern on page 23.)

Maya Noblewoman
dressed in elaborate
clothes and jewelry

Maya Peasant Woman and Child
Babies were strapped to boards to
elongate their heads. The Mayas
thought this made them more attractive.

Maya Peasant Woman Weaving
Women were weavers of cotton and maguey fabrics
used for clothing their families and for trade.

Maya Civilization Stand-Ups
(Use with stand pattern on page 23.)

Maya Warrior
A high ranking soldier wore more elaborate armor than other warriors.

Maya Batab
The governor was the highest ranking person in a city. He had supreme power over the people.

Maya Holpop
The judge settled disputes in the marketplace and decided on punishments.

Inca Civilization Stand-Ups

(Use with stand pattern on page 23.)

Inca Chosen Woman
A chosen woman was a priestess chosen for her beauty. She helped in ceremonies and made of the emperor's royal clothes.

Inca Peasant Woman 1
These women worked in the home caring for their families. She also helped her family in the farm and fields.

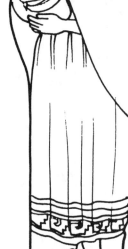

Inca Peasant Man
Men worked as traders or as farmers. Part of the year, they served the empire with community service as builders and soldiers.

Inca Civilization Stand-Ups

(Use with stand pattern on page 23.)

Inca Vicuna Herder
Herders kept vicunas for their wool
which was woven into fine fabric.

Inca Peasant Woman 2
Women were always busy. They spun wool
even when they were traveling.

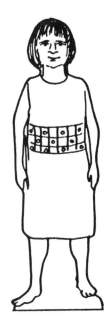

Inca Child
Children learned from their parents. They
went to school each evening to learn to
take part in dances and festivals.

Inca Runner
Runners took messages from
the emperor in Cuzco to
other Inca cities. They
memorized the messages to
relay to other runners.

Inca Civilization Stand-Ups

(Use with stand pattern on page 23.)

Inca Soldier
All able men served time in the army. They conquered cities for the emperor to add to the empire.

Inca Army Officer
Officers of high rank were blood relatives of the emperor. They led armies and conquered new lands for the empire.

Inca Priest
Priests were relatives of the emperor. They led ceremonies for Inti, the Sun God. It was believed that the emperor was the child of the sun.

Aztec Civilization Stand-Ups

(Use with stand pattern on page 23.)

Aztec Eagle Warrior
The warrior was known by his battle uniform.
The razor-sharp club had obsidian blades.

Aztec Jaguar Warrior
Warriors of poor rank could work their way up to
become part of the nobility of the empire. The
Jaguar and Eagle Warriors were the best.

Aztec Civilization Stand-Ups

(Use with stand pattern on page 23.)

Aztec Ball Player
This sacred game was played in honor of the gods. Only nobles or paid court players were allowed to play.

Aztec Ambassador
The ambassador was the agent of the king. He ordered conquered cities to pay *tribute* in gold, animal skins, and other items of value. Tribute was a sort of tax.

Aztec Warrior
Most soldiers wore padded cotton suits to protect them in battle. The stiff suit was almost an inch thick.

Aztec Civilization Stand-Ups

(Use with stand pattern on page 23.)

Aztecs Nobles
The rich nobles wore beautiful patterned clothes and jewelry. They also had fancy hairstyles.

Aztec Peasants
Peasants dressed in plain clothes. They worked as farmers and helped tradesmen with their crafts.

Aztec Children
By the time a child was three, he or she began learning household and farming chores. They learned by watching and imitating their parents.

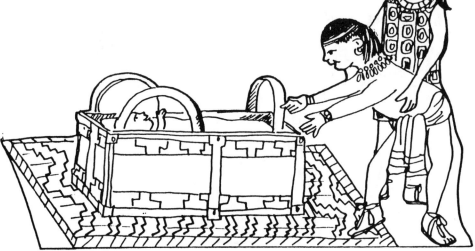

Civilization Stand-Ups

(Use with stand pattern on page 23.)

Maya Procession

Processions

Maya, Aztec, and Inca rulers were treated with great respect, almost as gods. They were carried on stretchers known as *litters*.

Aztec Procession

Inca Procession

Chapter 2

Art, Science, and Religion

The great Aztec calendar stone has glyphs which represent the days in an Aztec year. The calendar was used to predict eclipses.

33

Background Information for the Teacher

The **Maya** were highly cultured people with complex writing, mathematical, and astrological systems. Scholarly study of the Maya has increased with the deciphering of their glyphs. The Maya were the only people in ancient America to develop an original writing system, to make paper from trees, and to use paper to make books. Of thousands of codices or folding screen books, all but four were destroyed by the Spanish. The Maya invented a number system with the concept of zero long before it was understood in Europe. Pottery and walls are today's best examples of Maya painting, which were important to daily and ritual life of Maya society. Painters were highly educated and held positions of importance. Artists recorded history and mythology, one and the same with the Maya. Music and dancing were important in religious rituals and used to "contact" various gods.

Aztec civilization was not the true creation of the Aztecs. Their artistic, religious, and technical achievements were based on the more advanced cultures of the Toltecs, Mayas, and Zapotecs, earlier groups they conquered and displaced. Aztec culture combined elements of these earlier civilizations. They developed a culture that included a stone wheel calendar; sculptures in hard and soft stone; buildings made with exceptional engineering skills; and jewelry made of jade, turquoise, and other semiprecious stones. Metal work included copper, silver, and gold. We know more about their culture from their picture writing that still exists today and which is easier to interpret than that of the Maya.

Less is known about the great **Inca** empire because they had no form of writing and much of their culture was destroyed when the Spanish conquistadors took their gold and artifacts back to Spain. What we know we learned from their architectural ruins, pottery, and gravesites. The Incas erected massive buildings of stone that were so expertly cut that they needed no cement to hold them together. They built thousands of miles of roads and suspension bridges, many of which are still in use today. The highest of their many gods was Inti, the Sun God, who was worshiped with a festival at least once a month. The Incas were excellent weavers, potters, and metal workers.

Social Skills: Work cooperatively.
Academic Skills: Following directions. Keeping on task.
Teacher: Reproduce patterns and instructions for each group. Help students gather materials needed for projects.

Group Organization for Chapter 2 Projects

MATERIALS
- Look over the projects and choose the ones you'd like your class to do.
- Copy the intructions on bond paper and the patterns on oak tag.
- Organize instructions and patterns in three areas (for Maya, Aztec, and Inca) of the classroom.
- Assign and help children gather materials they will need. Groups can choose their projects and gather materials one day and complete the activity the next.
- Use self-hardening clay for the pottery and serpent mosaic projects. A good brand is AMOCO Mexican Pottery Self-Hardening Clay. Other clays can be ordered from Re-Print at 1-800-248-9171.

ORGANIZING GROUP PROJECTS
- Ask students to pick their spot: Maya, Aztec, or Inca.
- The projects use three types of cooperative groups: Pairs Check; Think, Write, Pair, Share; and Simultaneous Round Table. Group children in twos or fours according the the recipe heading at the top of the project page. See the Appendix (pages 97-109) for more information.
- Encourage groups to move on to other projects after they have completed the first one.
- Ask groups to reorganize and work on different projects for several days, so that different groups can experience a variety of activities.

EXTENSION ACTIVITIES
- **Extension Activity 1:** Groups gather and discuss what they learned and how they created it. Volunteers can stand before the class and explain the project.

- **Extension Activity 2:** When a group finishes one project, they can go on to another.

- **Extension Activity 3:** Groups can interview and learn from others who studied a different civilization.

Maya Codex

A Maya book is called a *codex*. Codices (plural) were parchments made from vegetable fibers mixed with a glue, and included writings about everyday life, religious ceremonies and gods, history, medicine, and astronomy. Only four codices still exist today. It is believed that the hundreds of codices that once existed were destroyed by the Spanish.

Materials
- butcher paper
- oak tag or cardboard
- glue
- markers
- scissors

To Make
1. Cut butcher paper 28" x 8" and two oak tag or cardboard pieces 7" x 8".
2. Fold the long sheet in half. Fold in half again.
3. Unfold the long sheet and refold on creases back and forth like a fan.
4. Glue oak tag or cardboard to front and back of folded codex pages.
5. Design a cover for the book and color it.
6. Your codex is now ready for you to write in. Perhaps you'd like to learn about Maya writing known as *heiroglyphs* (see next page).

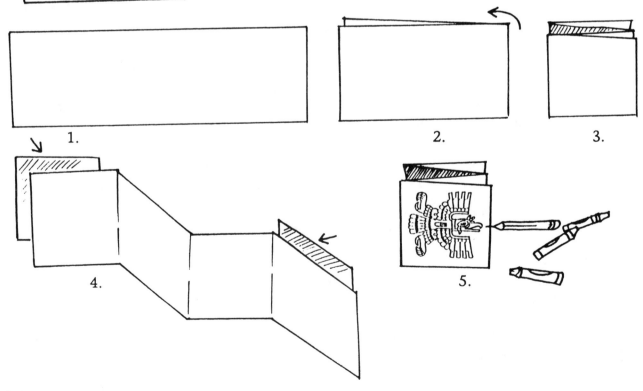

1.   2.   3.

4.   5.

Mayan Heiroglyphs

Mayas, the only ancient Central American people to develop a writing system, used picture symbols called *heiroglyphs*. Some heiroglyphs were made up of a main picture with elements added to it. These pictures allowed the Maya to express all their ideas. Heiroglyphs were shown on pottery, walls, codices, and ornaments. Scholars who have learned to decipher much of Maya writing, believe priests and nobles were the only people who could read the heiroglyphs.

Materials
- blank codex
- drawing paper
- markers
- scissors
- glue

To Make
1. With a partner write a short story about something that interests you both.
2. Create pictures (heiroglyphs) that illustrate the words in your story. Practice on drawing paper.
3. When you have completed your picture story, color it with markers, cut it out, and glue it onto a codex.

Aztec Writing

The Aztecs wrote in pictures: Some had symbolic meaning, but most pictures were literal, representing exactly what they were. When Aztec warriors conquered a village, they demanded that the citizens pay them taxes or a *tribute*, a list of goods they they expected to be given. The list of each town's tribute was listed in a codex made from deerskin or bark.

The codex page below lists a tribute that a village was required to give the Aztecs each year.
1. Discuss the pictures with a partner. Use your imaginations to decide what each symbol represents.
2. Make a list of what you think the list included and how many there are of each item.
3. Color the codex page, cut it out, and glue it into a codex along with your list.

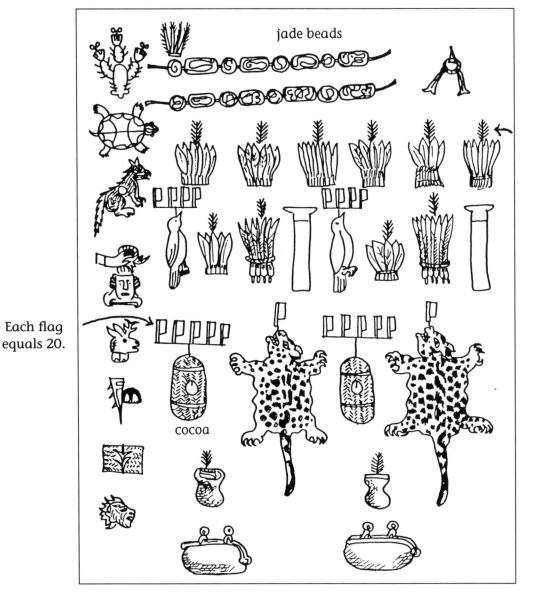

jade beads

The fir tree symbol equals 400.

Each flag equals 20.

cocoa

38

Aztec Counting

The Aztec number system was based on 20, rather than 10 like our system, and was composed of dots and flags. It also used the concept of zero which was uncommon in the number systems of that time.

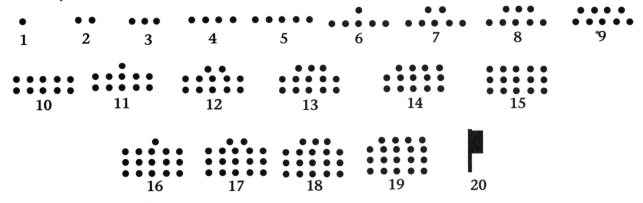

With a partner, write the numbers below in the Aztec way.

Dot = 1 **Flag = 20**

Example 23 = ▐ ••• (20 + 3)

28   46

14   65

81   37

32   60

Extension Activity: Each partner makes up math problems using the Aztec numbers. Partners trade papers and try to solve the other's math. Help each other check results.

Inca Quipu

Incas kept records of people, animals, tributes to be paid, etc. with a device known as the *quipu*. The quipu was a long cord held horizontally, to which a series of strings at different lengths, colors, and twists were attached. The accountants "read" the quipus and remembered what each string represented.

Materials
• 18" heavy cord or rope
• 3-23" pieces of string or yarn (in three different colors)
• scissors

Making the Quipu
Partners take turns completing each step and checking one another's work.

1. Hold the rope by both ends while your partner knots the yarn onto the rope.
2. Fold one piece of yarn in half. Then, fold the center loop of the yarn over the rope. Pull ends of yarn through the loop. Repeat with the other 2 pieces of yarn.

Example: 352

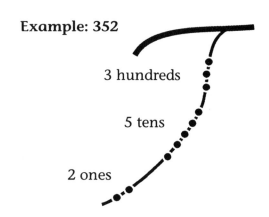

3 hundreds

5 tens

2 ones

Knotting the Quipu
Each partner knots three cords with the numbers shown below. See example:
• Knot **hundreds** on the cord near the rope.
• Knot **tens** in the center of the cord.
• Knot **ones** near the bottom of the cord.

With the help of a partner, represent the follwing numbers on your quipu.

1st color	2nd color	3rd color
231 llamas	564 warriors	174 jugs of corn
142 vicunas	273 shields	75 bags of potatoes

Extension Activity: Keep records of people and items in your classroom with your quipu. Add more yarn.

Aztec Calendar

This Aztec calendar was used to decide the times of festivals that occurred each year. Each day had a number from one to thirteen and one of twenty symbol names. This calendar is similar to the one used by the Maya.

Materials
- heavy cardboard
- white glue
- scissors
- markers
- 2 thumbtacks

Making the Calendar
1. Color the glyphs.
2. Glue both wheels to cardboard.
3. Cut them out.

Using the Calendar
1. Line up the wheels so that the point next to the rabbit is in the groove next to "one dot."
2. Tack them in place on a bulletin board.
3. The **left** wheel turns **clockwise**. The **right** wheel turns **counter-clockwise**.

Left Wheel

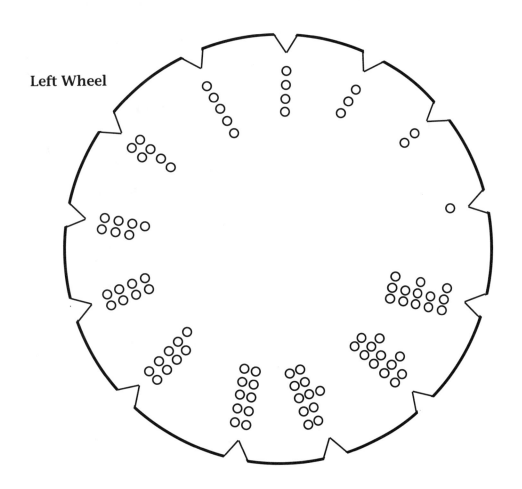

Right Wheel

Example:
- The first day of the year is 1– Rabbit.
- The second day of the year is 2– Water
- The third day is 3– Dog, etc.

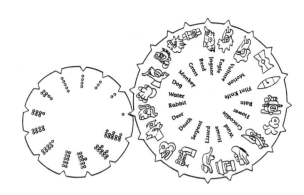

Assembly Diagram

 **Extension Activity:** Write the Aztec days of the month on a regular calendar. One person turns the calendar wheels and calls out the name of the Aztec day while the other writes the day on the calendar.

Feather Working

Bright tropical feathers from many colorful birds were valuable for trade, tribute, and use by the nobles of all three cultures. In most cases the birds were not killed for their feathers. They were captured, plucked, and let go. Feather pieces were status symbols like fancy cars or special clothes are today.

Maya Headdress

Maya feather workers made elaborate headdresses that hung to the ground in back and made wearers look like a bird that had just landed. The favored bird was the *quetzal* because of its long green tail feathers. Fans and cloaks were also popular.

Aztec warriors of high rank wore feather suits and headdresses and carried feather-covered shields. Skilled feather workers had high status and lived in their own section of the city. Feather garments could be worn only by the nobility, who liked quetzal feathers best.

Montezuma II Headdress

Inca Fan

Incas used feathers as part of their dress for special occasions. They also made fans, tunics, mosaics, and headdresses.

Inca Ruler Headdress

Materials
- bulky yarn in red, blue, and yellow
- black feather and white feather
- red tassel fringe (paper or cotton)
- scissors
- small piece of heavy aluminum foil
- glue

To Make
1. Cut four–36" pieces of each color of yarn.
2. Take one piece of each color and braid it loosely. Knot the ends of each braid. Make four braids.
3. Knot ends of all four braids together.
4. Cut the medallion from heavy duty aluminum foil.
5. Glue the feathers to center of the braids.
6. Glue the medallion over the feathers. Allow to dry.
7. Cut red paper or tassle fringe and glue behind medallion over feathers.
8. To wear, tie the braided ends at the back of the head.

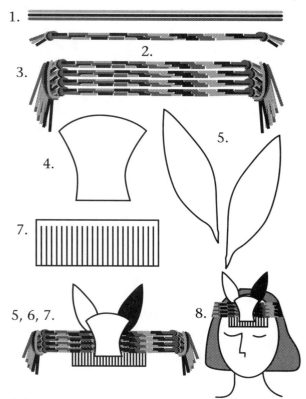

Maya Fan

Materials
- small, heavy white paper plate
- tongue depressor or ice cream stick
- markers
- green feathers (paper or real)
- glue

To Make
1. Color the plate first. The center of the plate is a butterfly within a red background.
2. The spokes are lines of red, blue, yellow, and green.
3. The arrow shaped lines are many alternating colors.
4. Color the edge of the plate red.
5. Glue green feathers underneath the outside edge of the plate.
6. Glue the tongue depressor or ice cream stick to the back of the plate.

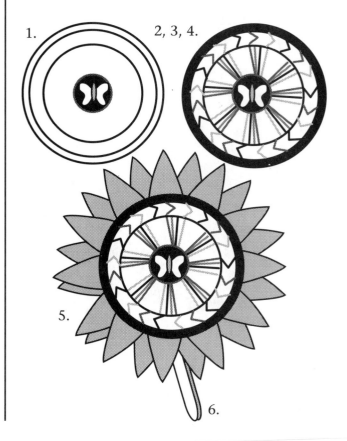

Masks

Almost every culture in the world has worn masks during festivals and ceremonies. The Incas, Aztecs, and Mayas were no exception. Masks were made of many materials, often inlaid with gold or gems. Masks were placed over mummies to protect them in the afterlife. Many were hung on walls in temples and worshiped.

Aztec Mosaic Mask Instructions

Materials
- mask, (page 46) copied on oak tag, 1 sheet
- coral construction paper, 1/2 sheet
- turquoise construction paper
- scissors
- white glue

To Make
1. Cut narrow 1/4" strips of of blue and coral paper. Cut strips into small pieces.
2. Glue the small pieces to the mask to cover the areas shown.

Assembly Diagrams

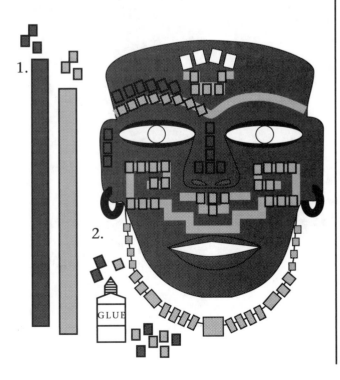

Inca Gold Sun-God Mask Instructions

Materials
- mask, (page 47) copied on oak tag
- white glue
- ballpoint pen
- gold foil
- scissors
- good quality paper towel

To Make
1. Glue the foil to the **back** of the mask pattern.
2. Turn the mask over so that the pattern shows.
3. Place the folded towel underneath the face to cushion the foil.
4. Using the ballpoint pen, trace the face crown patterns. Press hard and keep the paper towel under the foil as you work.
5. Cut out the mask.

Assembly Diagrams

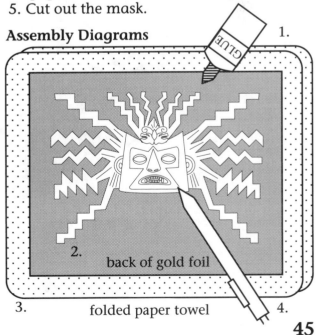

back of gold foil

folded paper towel

Aztec Mosaic Mask Pattern

Key

☐ shell

■ turquoise mosaic

▨ coral mosaic

To the Incas, gold was the "sweat of the sun" and silver was the "tears of the moon." This delicate gold mask may have hung in a temple or in an emperor's palace. It was believed that the emperor was descended from the sun god, **Inti**. Inti was the Inca's main god. He was served by many priests and priestesses. White llamas were sacrificed to him.

47

Pottery

All three societies made clay pottery for everyday household use and for religious ceremonies. None of the cultures used a potter's wheel. They rolled the clay in strips and coiled it into various shapes depending on its purpose. The method used for making the pottery and the decorations on it help scientists find out when it was made and by which culture.

Activity
Read the pottery descriptions below. Which pottery belongs to each culture? Partner with someone then discuss and give reasons for your decisions. Draw other pottery designs and explain why you think your design would belong with the Maya, Aztec, or Inca culture.

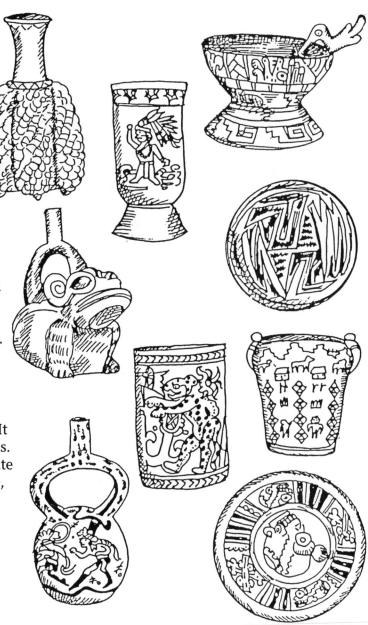

Maya pottery was usually of simple round cylinders and simple plates and bowls. Household pottery, used for cooking and water storage was plain. Ceremonial pottery had painted colorful scenes from Maya mythology or history.

Aztec potters decorated the inside of bowls with geometric designs painted in only two colors. It was made in simple shapes. Sometimes the decoration was cut into the surface rather than painted.

Inca pottery, called imperial Cuzco, is one of the culture's best achievements. It had many shapes and elaborate designs. Four or more colors were used to decorate the pottery. Designs had stylized people, animals, birds, and plants. Pots with stirrup spouts held chicha beer used to make offerings at religious ceremonies. Since Incas had no form of writing, pottery is valuable in learning about their ideas and culture.

Pottery Making

Pottery decorations were painted, carved, or stamped onto the clay. Choose a project below to complete with your partner.

Two-Color Design

Materials
- paper and pencil
- plain plastic margarine tub
- permanent black or red marker
- large, unfolded paper clip

To Make
1. Draw a simple design on paper.
2. Color the entire outside of the tub with the marker and allow to dry.
3. Using the paper clip, carefully scratch off the color to make your design.

Carved Design

Materials
- paper and pencil
- clay
- unfolded paper clip
- dull pencil
- clean, 14 1/2 oz. can

To Make
1. Draw a design on a 4 1/4" x 11" of paper using glyphs or other designs you have learned about.
2. Pat out a block of clay that is 4 1/4" x 11" x 1/4" thick.
3. "Cut" your design into the clay using the paper clip and pencil. Take out clay around the design so that it has a raised effect.
4. Wrap the clay around the can. Press to seal the edges together. Allow to dry thoroughly.

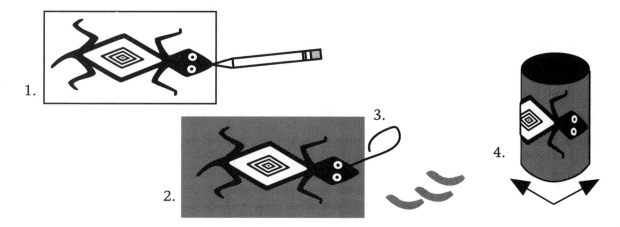

Maya Dance of Reeds

Dances and games were performed in the Dance Court near the temple or in the market place. The Maya Dance of Reeds was performed by as many as 150 people at a time. All three empires used dance to celebrate festivals and religious rites.

Materials
- warrior's headdress from page 92
- cloak from page 87
- wooden drum or tom-tom and drum sticks
- rattles (Mayas used gourd rattles)
- jingle bells (Mayas wore copper bells on the knees)

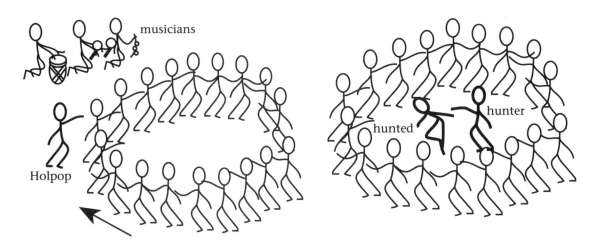

The Dance (for 10 or more)
1. One person is chosen to be the *holpop* (judge) and wears the headdress and cloak. He holds the spear.
2. The musicians beat out smooth rhythms with the drum, rattles, and bells. The drummer sets the tempo for the other musicians.
3. All dancers stand in a wide circle.
4. As the musicians play a steady rhythm, the dancers in the circle put their right hand on the next person's shoulder and move to the right in time to the music.
5. The holpop walks around the inside of the circle as the dancers move around. He taps one dancer on the shoulder (hunter) and taps another dancer on the shoulder (hunted). They move to the center of the circle and continue to dance in time to the music.
6. When the holpop claps his hands, the hunter tries to tag the hunted who tries to evade the hunter. If the hunted is tagged, he becomes the hunter and the other dancer returns to the circle. The holpop chooses another dancer to be the hunted.
7. The drummer can change the beat to speed or slow the dance.

Serpent Sculpture Mosaic

The double headed serpent probably represented Tlaloc, the Aztec god that signified the coming and going of rain. It was carved of wood and inlaid with turquoise and shells.

Materials
- serpent pattern from page 52
- red poster board (8"x 10")
- self drying clay
- plastic knives
- fettuccine pasta
- blue and green food coloring
- white vinegar
- paper towels
- plastic sandwich bags
- 2 white buttons or dried beans

Dyeing Fettuccine
1. Break eight to ten strands of fettuccine into tiny rectangles.
2. Mix one cup cold water, two teaspoons white vinegar, and one third bottle of food blue coloring.
3. Put fettuccine pieces into the colored mixture and allow to absorb dye until they are the desired color.
4. Drain pasta on paper towels. Allow to dry completely.
5. Store each color separately in plastic bags.

Assembly Diagrams

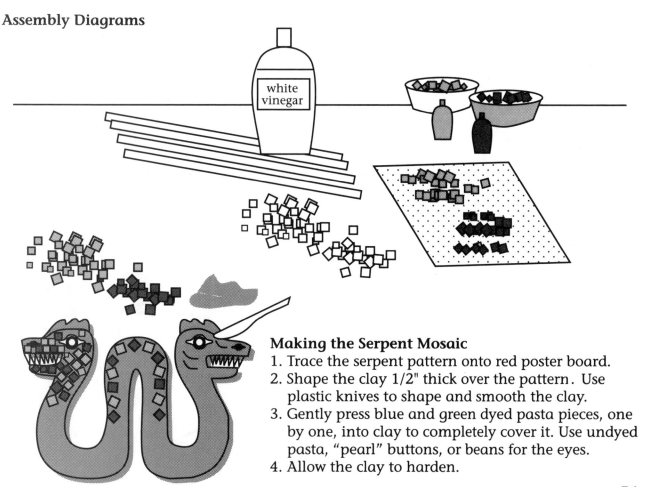

white vinegar

Making the Serpent Mosaic
1. Trace the serpent pattern onto red poster board.
2. Shape the clay 1/2" thick over the pattern. Use plastic knives to shape and smooth the clay.
3. Gently press blue and green dyed pasta pieces, one by one, into clay to completely cover it. Use undyed pasta, "pearl" buttons, or beans for the eyes.
4. Allow the clay to harden.

Serpent Pattern

Chapter 3

Family and Community

The Aztecs and Maya believed that gods were present during all activities. The figure in the upper left is believed to be the patron god, Macuilxochitl (Five Flower) watching over a game of Patolli.

For the Teacher

For the **Maya**, the heirarchy had feudal lords who received tribute (produce and services) from the peasants. The nobility did not pay tribute. At the marketplace, the center of the community, every sort of good was traded. Families brought crops and manufactured goods to market to barter for the goods they could not produce for themselves. The husband was responsible for the well-being of his family and his government. The wife was in charge of the household, which included weaving, cooking, and raising children. Girls learned domestic chores from their mothers and boys learned their father's trade. Children went to school to learn dances, songs, and about religious festivals. Noble children had their own schools where they learned, astrology, how to read codices, and how to rule.

The **Aztec** way of life was very similar to that of the Maya. People paid tribute to the government in the form of food, clothing, skins, gold, silver, and feathers–whatever the family was able to hunt, trade or produce themselves.

The **Inca** emperor, supported by the aristocracy, had supreme rule over the entire culture. Each family was alloted land and homes, according to their needs. In return, they gave a portion of their crop to the state: the emperor, other nobles, and the army. The crops collected were consumed or stored for use during the seasons of poor crop production. In conquered territories local officials kept their jobs, but had to support the Inca system. Government officials strictly enforced social and moral codes. They even went from house to house to check that women kept their homes clean. "Mita" was a from of work tax all married farmers had to pay. Nobles did not do mita service.

Group Organization for Chapter 3

Pages 56 – 61: Mural Scenes and Facts

 Social Skills: Seek accuracy, integrate ideas into a whole, work toward goal.
Academic Skills: Use mapping skills to create a cooperative large-scale mural of an ancient scene.
Teacher: This is a repeat of the mural drawing activity described on pages 15 and 16 in Chapter 1. Follow the same directions for pages 56 to 61.

Pages 62 – 67: Rain Forest Hunt Game

 Social Skills: Elaborate, speak clearly, integrate ideas into a single conclusion.
Academic Skills: Learn the reasons ancient peoples hunted, what they hunted, and some of their ancient weapons through game play.
Teacher: Reproduce game components on oak tag. Help children find references for coloring the rain forest animals. For extended use, laminate the playing pieces after they have been colored.

Pages 68 – 69: Inca Embroidery

 Social Skills: Divide tasks quickly and quietly.
Academic Skills: Follow directions in cutting and pasting to complete task.
Teacher: Reproduce several patterns for each group.

Pages 70 and 71: Maya or Aztec Dugout Canoe, Inca Reed Boat

 Social Skills: Divide tasks, use eye contact, participate actively.
Academic Skills: Follow directions to build a miniature boat.
Teacher: Reproduce directions for each group and provide materials. Some students may be too young to carve the dugout canoe. If you agree, omit this activity.

Pages 72 – 75: Trade, Tribute, and Sacrifice Game

Social Skills: Cooperate quietly while trading, ask for help when needed.
Academic Skills: Recognize and compare categories of goods and products.
Teacher: Reproduce the co-op cards on pages 12, 13, 14, 74, and 75 on oak tag for each group. Cut cards apart. Reproduce one game board for each player in each group and one cube and one set of Tribute and Sacrifice boards for each group.

Pages 76: Patolli Game

 **Social Skills:** Elaborate, speak clearly, integrate ideas into a single conclusion.
Academic Skills: Create a game and play it successfully. Teach another group to play.
Teacher: Reproduce and enlarge game board on oak tag.

Maya Market Place

Thousands of people traded in city markets each day.

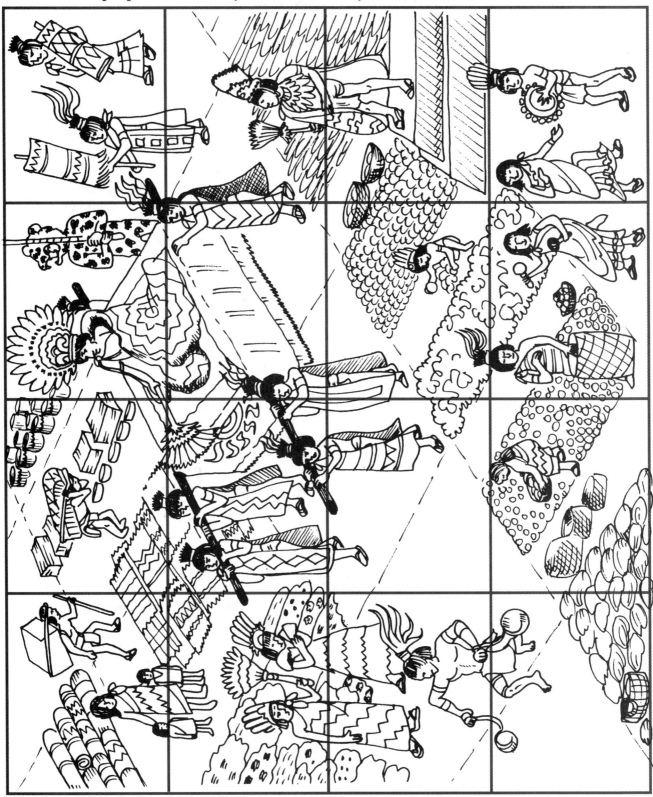

Maya Market Place Facts

Cut facts apart and put them around your mural. String colored cord between fact cards and the areas the card describes. Research library books to get more facts about Maya markets.

1. The nobility was in charge of all trade between cities. Ambassadors traveled hundreds of miles to cities that had goods that their city needed.

2. Goods traded included cotton, salt, honey, wax, slaves, weapons, cacao, precious metals, baskets, all sorts of food, and feathers.

4. At the market, people traded news as well as goods they had made or needed.

3. Each product traded in a market had a specific place. All the pottery or weapons were placed in their own areas.

6. A judge walked among the traders or stood watch over everyone to make sure that each person was treated fairly.

5. Musicians and dancers entertained people at the market. Plays were also performed.

7. People carried all goods on their backs. The Maya had no animals large enough to carry heavy loads.

8. The governor of a city or other nobles were carried through the market in processions. Common people were not allowed to look directly at the governor.

Aztec Family Life

Most Aztec families lived in small houses near the fields where their crops grew.

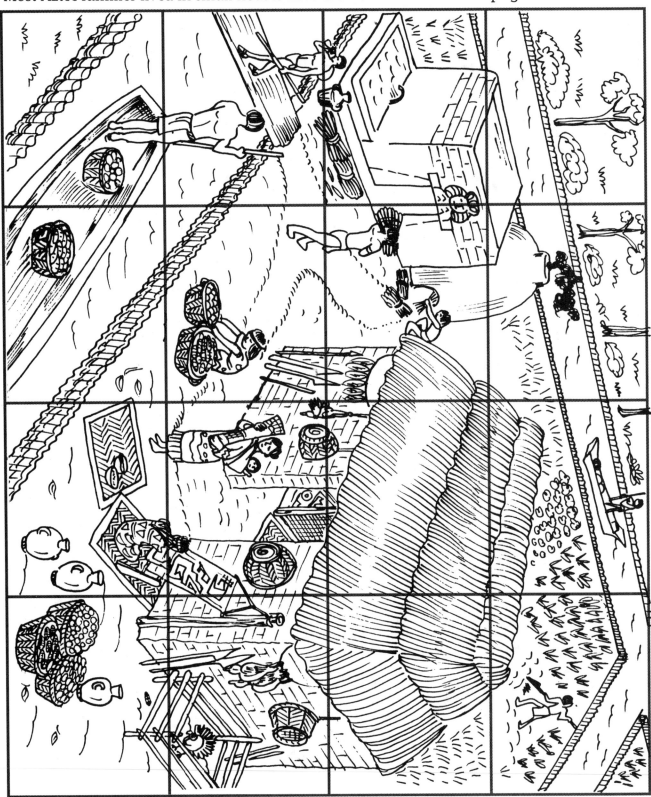

Aztec Family Life Facts

Cut facts apart and put them around your mural. String colored cord between fact cards and the areas the card describes. Research library books to get more facts about Aztec family life.

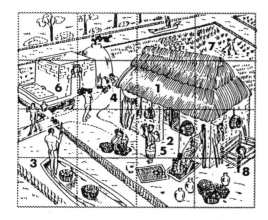

1. Most homes were made of *adobe* (mud bricks). Houses had pitched, thatched roofs with brightly painted walls.

2. Aztec homes had two rooms: one for sleeping, and one for living and eating. The only furniture were reed mats for sleeping and wooden storage chests. Food was cooked on a stone grate.

3. Trade goods were often put into baskets and taken to market in dug-out canoes.

4. Since the houses were so small, many possessions were hung on outside walls. Much work, such as weaving, was done outside. Girls learned about household chores from their mothers.

5. There were no windows in the house and only one door. Fires used for cooking and for light kept the houses smoky.

6. The Aztecs took steam baths in a small separate building beside the house. Bathing was done for cleanliness and for ritual religious reasons.

7. Food for the family was grown in gardens called *chinampas*. Boys helped their fathers in the fields and learned other trades. Fathers passed on their professions to their sons.

8. Aztec families raised animals for food. Turkey was a favorite, but they also enjoyed eating small dogs called chihuahuas.

Inca Farmers and Builders

Inca farmers were expected to erect roads and buildings.

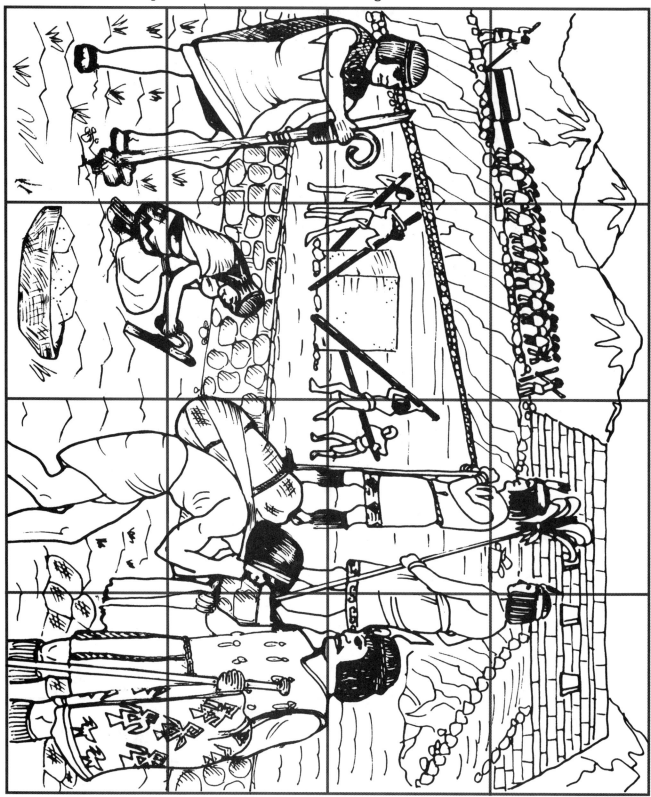

 # Inca Farmers and Builders Facts

Cut facts apart and put them around your mural. String colored cord between fact cards and the areas the cards describe. Research library books to get more facts about Incas.

1. All married farmers had to spend part of their time erecting buildings or roads. This was called *mita* service. It was a form of paying taxes. Nobles, priests, and emperors did not pay taxes.

2. The Incas did not have the wheel. They rolled huge building stones into place on large log rollers. Some stones weighing many tons, were pulled for more than eighteen miles.

3. Mita workers built excellent roads and huge buildings of stone. The stones fit together so well that no mortar was necessary. Many of the stone walls they built are still standing today after hundreds of years and many earthquakes.

4. Families were given land to farm according to their needs. When a new baby was born to a family, they were given more land to farm.

6. Farmers kept part of their crop. The rest went to the emperors (for use during bad crop years), to the priests, and the armies.

5. Both men and women worked in the fields. They used digging sticks and hoes to till the land. Farmers terraced their fields in the mountains to keep from losing soil and to irrigate crops.

7. Government workers kept records of what farmers took to storehouses. Most government workers were relatives of the royal family.

8. Members of the royal family and high ranking army officers reported everything they saw to the emperor. If unrest occurred, armies were sent in to settle disputes and to keep control of each city in the empire.

Rain Forest Hunt Game

a game for 2–6 players

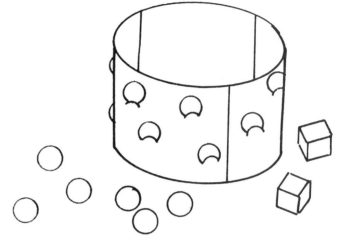

Game Components
- game board on pages 63, 64, 65
- cubes on page 66
- play pieces on page 67

To Make the Game
1. Color the game board scenes.
2. Cut out game board pieces and the slits on the solid lines near each animal. Tape or glue the pieces together to make a round stand-up game scene.
3. Cut out the Reason and Weapon cubes. Assemble as shown on page 66.
4. Cut out the game play pieces.

Game Play
1. The object of the game is to "hunt" animals for a specific reason with a specific weapon. Players must remember why each animal is captured to win the game.
2. Each player gets four game pieces with the same animal motif.
3. The first player rolls the two cubes and reads the reason for hunting an animal and the weapon that must be used.
4. The player then picks an animal on the round game board that could be hunted for that reason and with that weapon. The player must state his or her intent, and name how and why the animal is captured.
5. When the player has chosen an animal to "hunt," he or she places one of the game pieces in the slit below the animal. That animal can not be hunted again.
6. Play continues with each player taking turns rolling the cubes and placing game pieces on the board. If a player can not match an animal with the reason and weapon rolled, he or she does not place a game piece on the board.
7. A player who has placed all four of his or her game pieces on the board is the winner.

Rain Forest Hunt Game Board

Rain Forest Hunt Game Board

Glue game board together here.

jaguar

capybara

woolly monkey

peccary

agouti

quetzal

hanging parrot

toucan

capuchin monkey

armadillo

Rain Forest Hunt Game Board

Glue game board together here.

howler monkey

roseate spoonbill

fish

ocelot

marsh deer

salamander

otter

sloth

hyacinth macaw

marine toad

65

Rain Forest Game Cubes

(tuck flap inside)

Food

Reason Cube

| Tribute | Feathers | Trade | Skins |

(tuck flap inside)

Sacrifice

(tuck flap inside)

(tuck flap inside)

Net

Weapon Cube

| Knife | Arrow | Spear | Trap |

(tuck flap inside)

Club

(tuck flap inside)

To Make
1. Cut out the cubes.
2. Fold on dotted lines.
3. Tuck small flaps inside cube.
4. Tape edges to secure.

Rain Forest Hunt Game Pieces

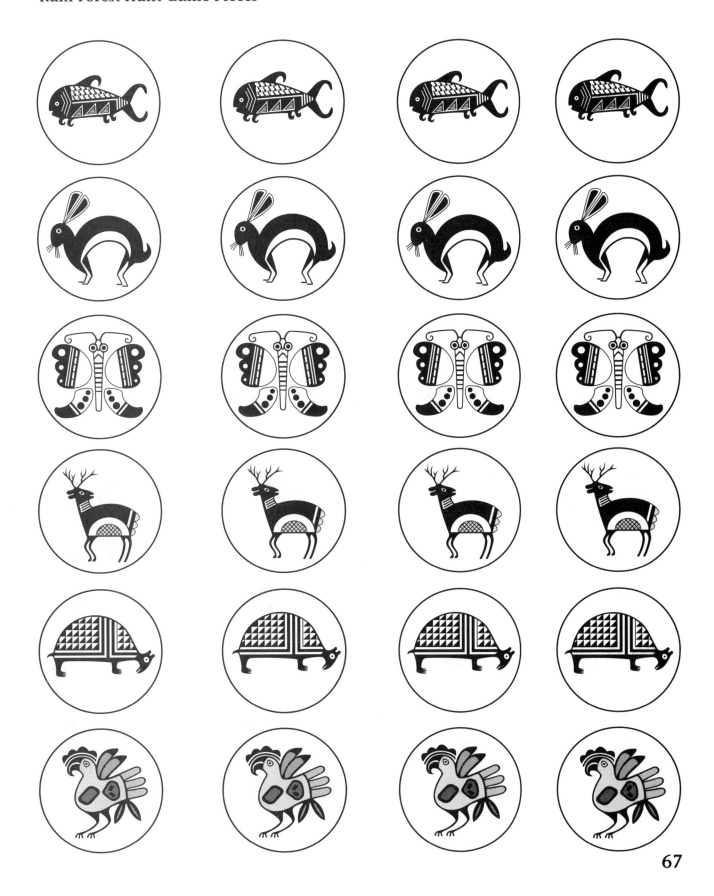

67

Inca Embroidery

All three groups were excellent weavers and spinners, but the Incas were masters at textile embroidery. You and your group can pretend to be Inca weavers by using the patterns provided.

Materials
- 5 different colors of construction paper, including black
- scissors
- glue

To Make
1. Trace and cut the rectangular shape (outside line) of the pattern on black contruction paper.
2. Cut the black zigzags from pattern below.
3. Trace and cut zigzags on colored paper. Each zigzag should be a different color.
4. Glue colored zigzag designs on black rectangle.

Embroidery Design 1

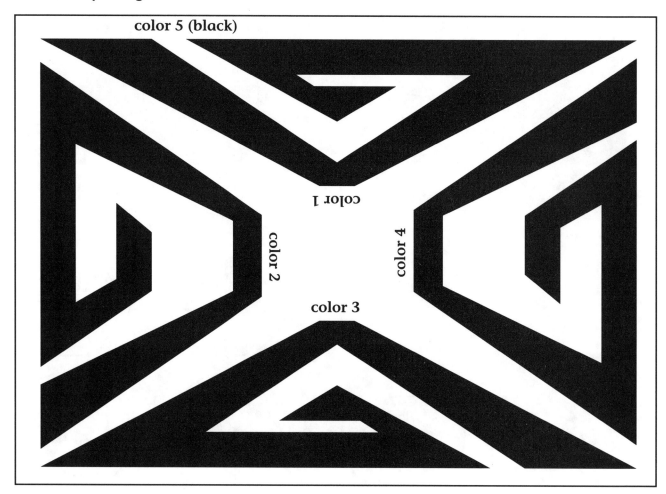

Embroidery Design 2

Materials
- 4 sheets of construction paper (each a different color)
- scissors
- glue

Cutter 1 cuts outside circle using color 1, and glues all layers.

Cutter 2 cuts inside black line of outside circle using color 2.

Cutter 3 cuts on black line of spoked circle using color 3.

Cutter 4 cuts on gray spoked circle using color 4.

Cutter 1 cuts outside black circle using color 1.

Cutter 2 cuts outside gray circle using color 2.

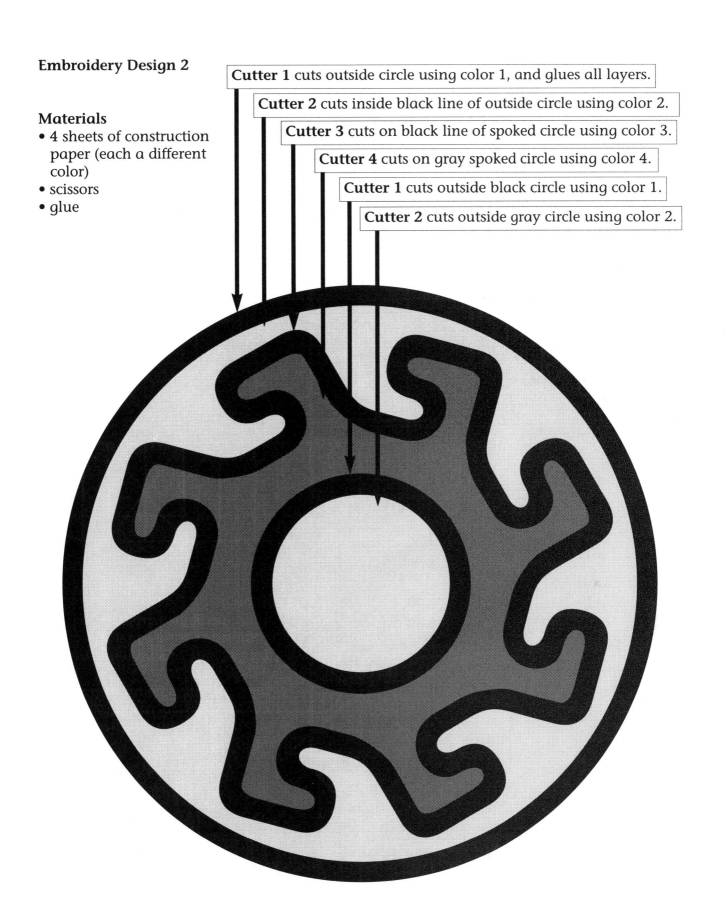

Maya or Aztec Dugout Canoe

The Mayas and the Aztecs made their boats by burning and digging out large trees. Royal canoes were carved and painted with glyphs and pictures of gods.

Materials
- block of balsa wood 3" x 8" x 1" thick
- pencil
- carving tools
- permanent markers or paints
- (optional) oven-fire clay (Sculpey® or Fimo® brand)
- (optional) cardboard or stick boat paddle

Carving the Canoe

1. Mark areas to cut away on front and back of balsa wood block. Cut the wood away. (see below)

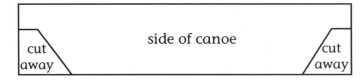

2. Dig out wood from inside the canoe to 1/4" thickness.

```
inside of canoe
cut out to 1/4" thickness
```

3. Paint the sides of the canoe.
4. Model optional miniature person out of oven-fire clay. Use a stick or painted cardboard for a paddle.

Note to teacher: Since this activity requires the use of sharp objects, it is recommended that you supervise.

Inca Reed Boat

The Incas used reeds that grew along Lake Titicaca to make boats for fishing and for sailing. People there today still make and use reed boats the same way the Incas once did.

1. and 2.

Materials
- craft raffia
- ruler
- scissors
- (optional) oven-fire clay (Sculpey® or Fimo® brand)
- (optional) cardboard or stick boat paddles

3.

To Make
1. Cut 45 12" pieces of raffia.
2. Lay 40 pieces side by side. Keep five pieces for tying.
3. Pinch the 40 pieces of raffia together at one end. Wrap one of the tying pieces around the tip, tying and tucking the end into the bunch.
4. Bunch the other end of the raffia together, pulling one edge of the raffia tighter to create a curving shape. Wrap another piece of 12" raffia around the other tip, tying and tucking ends in place.
5. Use the three remaining pieces of raffia to add shape to the boat by weaving them into the center and at the sides of the boat. Weave in and out of four or five pieces of raffia at a time, pulling each stitch tightly. Keep weaving each piece until ends are tucked into place and boat is shaped as shown.
6. Model optional miniature people out of oven-fire clay. Use sticks or painted cardboard for paddles.

4. (pull inner pieces tighter)

5.

Note: Use the boat for display only. The raffia boat will not float in water.

6.

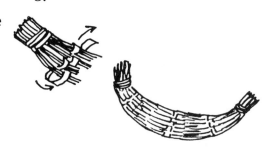

Extension Activity: Change the directions and craft materials to create a reed-type boat that *will* float. Keep a chart of the various materials used by groups, what they were made of, and how long each boat floated.

Trade, Tribute, and Sacrifice Game

Getting Ready to Play

1. Each player gets a game board below.
2. Shuffle all the Co-Op Cards together (from pages 12, 13, 14, 74, and 75).
3. Deal four cards face down to each player.
4. Place the rest of the deck face down in the center of the playing area.
5. Put Tribute and Sacrifice squares next to deck.

Playing the Game

1. After the cards are dealt, the first player rolls the cube (on page 73) and follows the directions on it.
2. **Trade a Card:** exchange a card with player on the right.
   Pay Tribute: place a card on the Pay Tribute square.
   Sacrifice a Card: place a card on the Sacrifice square.
   Draw a Card: draw a card fro the deck.
3. After following directions, a player may put **one** of the remaining cards on his or her game board if there is a space for it. If not, play passes to the next player.
4. The play continues until one person has covered his or her game board.

Game Board

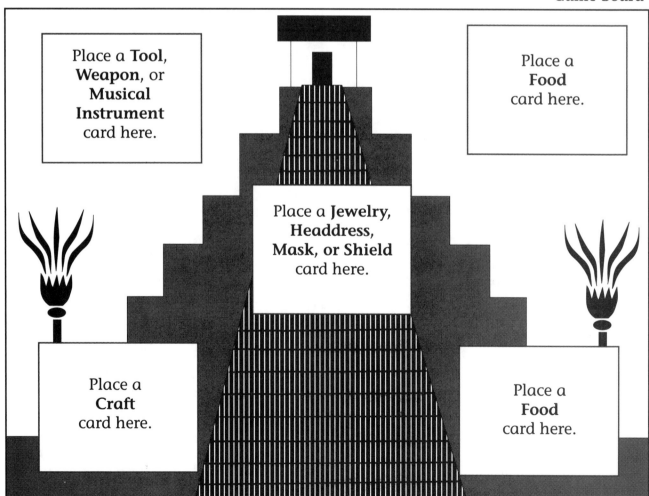

Place a **Tool, Weapon,** or **Musical Instrument** card here.

Place a **Food** card here.

Place a **Jewelry, Headdress, Mask, or Shield** card here.

Place a **Craft** card here.

Place a **Food** card here.

Trade, Tribute, and Sacrifice Game

Pay Tribute Here

Pay Tribute Here

Pay Tribute Here

Pay Tribute Here

Sacrifice a Card Here

Sacrifice a Card Here

Sacrifice a Card Here

Sacrifice a Card Here

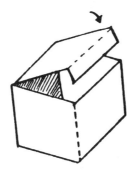

(tuck flap inside)

Trade a Card

(tuck flap inside)

| **Trade a Card** | **Pay Tribute** | **Sacrifice a Card** | **Draw a card** |

Draw a Card

(tuck flap inside)

To Make
1. Cut out the cube.
2. Fold on dotted lines.
3. Tuck small flaps inside cube.
4. Tape edges to secure.

Foods

The Mayas, Aztecs, and Incas generally ate two meals each day. The common people ate mostly fruits and vegetables and little meat. The nobles and emperors ate very lavish meals with lots of variety and many courses. Use these cards with the Trade, Tribute, and Sacrifice game beginning on page 72.

Maya, Aztec, Inca Foods Co-Op Cards

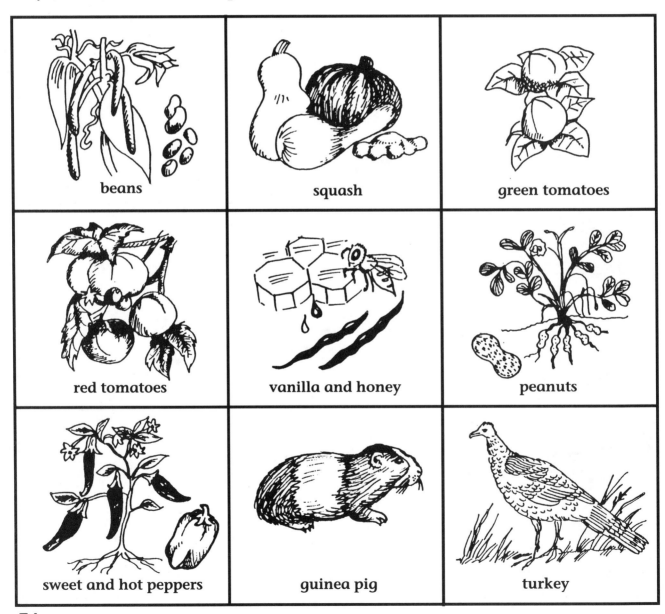

beans	squash	green tomatoes
red tomatoes	vanilla and honey	peanuts
sweet and hot peppers	guinea pig	turkey

cactus leaves	dog	avocadoes
llama	corn	potatoes
cacao (chocolate)	rabbit	duck
fish and shellfish	deer	tropical fruits, melons

Patolli Game

Patolli was a favorite board game of the Mayas and Aztecs, and very similar to our games of backgammon and parcheesi. Beans were tossed like dice and stones were moved around the board. Feathers and jewelry were wagered on the game.

Materials
- game board
- color marker pens
- 2 dice
- 4 different game markers or buttons

Playing the Game
1. Discuss how your game will be played and write the rules.
2. Color the game board with markers.
3. Test the play of your game and change any rules when necessary.
4. Share the game with another group.

Patolli Game Board

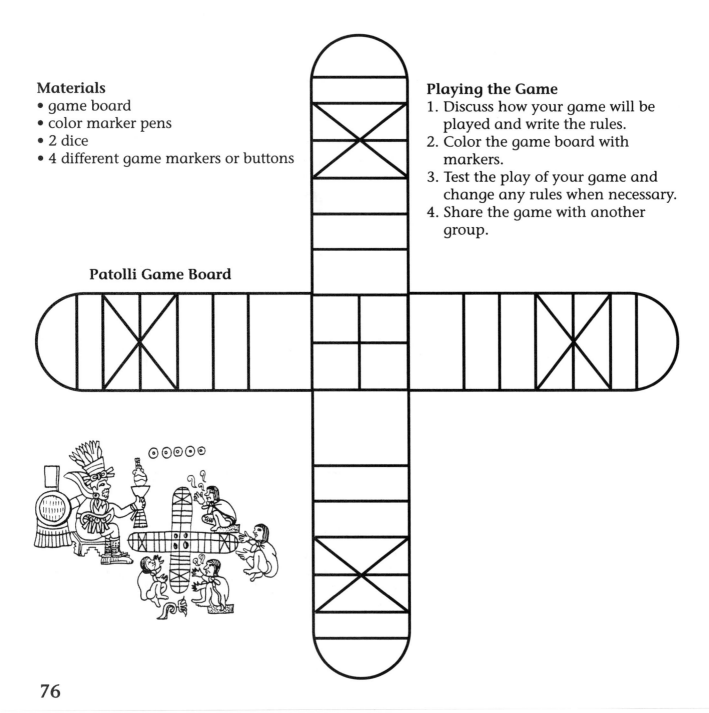

Chapter 4

The Flame of Peace
a tale of the Aztecs

For the Teacher

The Flame of Peace by Deborah Nourse Lattimore is a beautiful storybook retelling an Aztec myth about a boy who saves his city from war. The art is done in the ancient style. Many objects in the story are shown as hieroglyphs depicting animals, crops, and items for trade. Read the story with your class. Discuss the art style and what the glyphs depict. (The inside front and back covers have charts.) Introduce your study of these ancient cultures to your students by helping them convert the story into a stage play.

This chapter contains group activities for writing scripts, constructing scenery, and making props and costumes in the Aztec style. Encourage students to use the patterns only as a guide for creating what they need. They should feel free to decorate items based on the art in the book. You may want to combine efforts with another class; with one class writing the script and assigning and learning roles, while the other class creates the sets and costumes.

Group Organization

After your discussion of the story, divide the class into groups of two to write the script and make the props. The story has been divided into 14 scenes. The first task will be writing the script in play form based on the words in the story. After the the whole script is complete, assign roles for speaking and non-speaking parts.

Divide the class again into new groups of two to make the scenery, props, and costumes for each scene. There are many patterns on the following pages to help groups with their designs. Writing the script and making props for the play should take several days.

When you stage the play, the narrator will read his part at the side of the stage while others enter and exit as needed. Non-speaking actors can move the scenery and props on and off the stage.

Writing the Script: Copy one set of **Scene Strips** on pages 79 and 80. Divide the class into groups of two, and copy and hand out one **Script Writing Sheet** to each group. Each group and then describe and write the dialogue for that scene. Children not familiar with scriptwriting might request your help. See example provided below.

> **Script Example** (from Scene 1):
> **Narrator:** Emperor Itzcoatl himself appears before the temple, draped in his imperial robes.
> **Emperor** (enters scene and says): Tezozomoc and his army are in the hills. He plans to capture our city.

Setting the Scene: Copy one set of **Scene Strips** on pages 79 and 80. Copy and hand out one **Scene Planning Sheet** on page 82 to each group. Also, copy several sets of the patterns for props, costumes, and scenery for each group.

Scene Strips

Reproduce, cut apart, and give each group two copies of one strip. The strip is glued to the Script Writing Sheet on page 81 and to the Scene Planning Sheet on page 82. Starred characters (*) have speaking parts.

Scene 1: (pages 4–7)	**Characters:** *Narrator *Emperor Warriors Two Flint	**Props:** Fishing basket Battle Flags Costumes
Scene 2: (pages 8–12)	**Characters:** *Five Eagle *Narrator *Two Flint Dancers Ambassadors *Emperor	**Props:** Gifts Conch shells Copal Juice
Scene 3: (pages 13–15)	**Characters:** *Two Flint Foot runners *One Flower Warriors *Narrator	**Props:** Home Bowls Torches
Scene 4: (pages 16–17)	**Characters:** *Lord Morning Star Warriors *Narrator *One Flower Two Flint	**Props:** Bed Weapons Costumes
Scene 5: (pages 18–20)	**Characters:** *Two Flint *Crossroads	**Props:** Sound effect Road Sun River Costume
Scene 6: (page 21)	**Characters:** *Two Flint *Narrator *Lord River	**Props:** Sound effect Waterspout Costume
Scene 7: (pages 22–23)	**Characters:** *Two Flint *Lord River *Lord Wind	**Props:** Sound effect Costume

Scene Strips

Scene 8: (pages 24–25)	**Characters:** *Two Flint *Wind *Lord Storm	**Props:** Sound effect Riverbank Storm's frogs
Scene 9: (pages 26–27)	**Characters:** *Two Flint *Earthquake	**Props:** Sound effect Tree
Scene 10: (pages 28–29)	**Characters:** *Two Flint *Lord Volcano *Narrator	**Props:** Sound effect Flames Cape Cave Blanket
Scene 11: (pages 30–31)	**Characters:** *Lord Smoking Mirror *Two Flint *Narrator	**Props:** Sound effect Rock statue Cloak of Forgetfulness
Scene 12: (pages 32–33)	**Characters:** *Two Flint *Lady Death *Lord Death *Narrator	**Props:** Sound effect
Scene 13: (pages 34–35)	**Characters:** *Two Flint *Lord Morning Star	**Props:** Hill of the Star Music Flowers Torch
Scene 14: (pages 36–40)	**Characters:** *Two Flint *Emperor Warriors *Narrator	**Props:** Marketplace Altar

Script Writing Sheet

Work together to write a script for your scene in the play. Remember to add notes about what the actors are to do in the scene. Add another sheet, if needed.

Glue your Scene Strip here.

Script Writers: _____

Setting: _____

_____

Script: _____

_____

_____

_____

_____

_____

_____

_____

_____

_____

_____

_____

Scene Planning Sheet

Work together to plan your scene in the play. Add another sheet, if needed.

> Glue your Scene Strip here.

Prop Technician: _____ **Costume Designer:** _____

Sound Effects: (and how to do them) **Costumes Needed:**

_____ _____

_____ _____

_____ _____

Props Needed:

_____

_____

_____

Actors in the Play:

_____

_____

_____

Setting the Scene

Use the illustrations below to decorate the stage for your play. Your group may wish to make the scenery less or more elaborate.

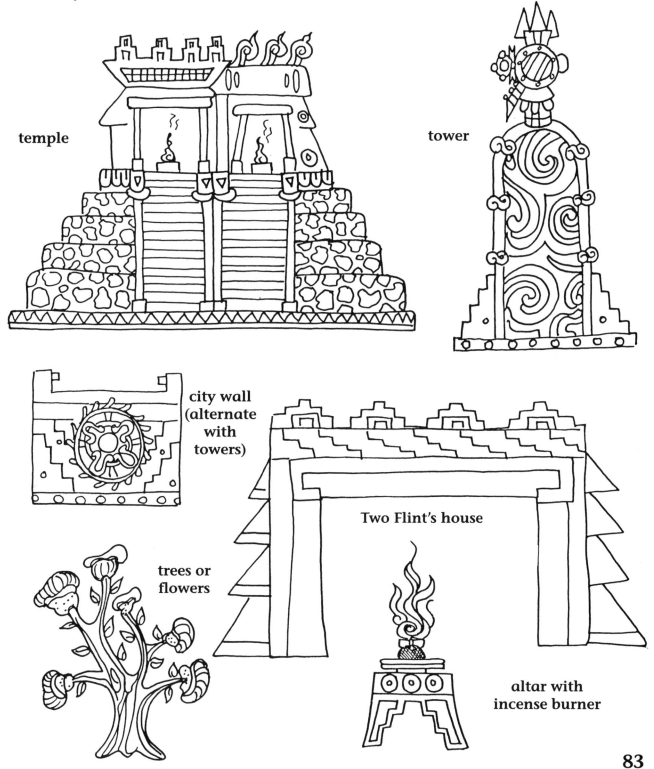

temple

tower

city wall
(alternate
with
towers)

Two Flint's house

trees or
flowers

altar with
incense burner

Setting the Scene

These pages have ideas for making some of the things you need for your play. Your group may decide to use their own ideas. Look closely at the art in *The Flame of Peace* to ensure props match the colors and styles of the Aztecs.

Two Flint's Fishing Basket

A cornucopia basket often used in table decorations during Thanksgiving would make a good fishing basket. If that is not available, make a cone shape from a large piece of brown paper. Draw, color, and cut out fishes to "catch" in the basket.

The River

You need a river for Two Flint to fish in at the beginning of the play and when Lord River tries to stop him in scenes 6 and 7.

Materials
- rolls of crepe paper streamers in two shades of blue
- scissors
- 2 yard sticks
- masking tape

To Make
1. Cut the streamers in 6' lengths.
2. Tape the streamers to each of the dowels or yard sticks with masking tape.

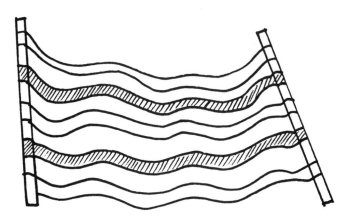

To Use: Two dancers crouch and face each other while holding one end of the river. They wave the yard sticks up and down to simulate water flowing.

City Walls and Tower

Three groups are needed to paint the walls and tower. Decide on designs for each piece by looking at the art on pages 6, 7, and 36 in *The Flame of Peace*. The walls are low rectangles. The tower is a tall rectangle.

Materials
- plain paper
- 3 large sheets of corrugated board
- pencils
- tempera paints
- brushes

To Make
1. Work together to draw your design on paper.
2. Draw the design in pencil on the corrugated board.
3. Paint the designs and allow them to dry.

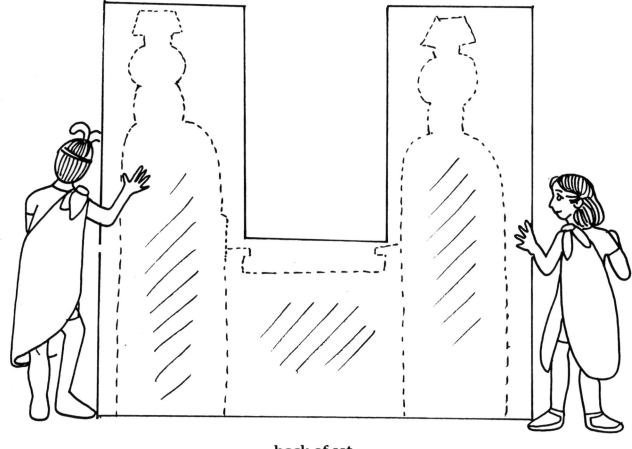

back of set

To Use: Dancers hold the walls and tower in position during the play.

Costumes

Wear plain gym shorts and a tee shirts under simple costumes. Emperors dressed elaborately while servants dressed plainly. Decorate the costumes with paints or paper cutouts.

Loin Cloth

Male Aztecs wrapped these around the waist and between the legs. Use these for most of the actors in the play including Two Flint and other male players.

Materials
- bath towel or piece of plain cloth
- safety pins
- several colors of oak tag
- scissors
- glue

To Make
1. Make an ornament for the front of the loin cloth using different colors of oak tag.
2. Cut various geometric shapes and designs. See examples below.
3. Glue the shapes in layers with the largest on the bottom and the smallest on the top.

To Wear: Wrap the towel around the waist, using a safety pin to secure it. Pin the ornament to the front of the "loin cloth" at the waist.

Cloak or Cape

The Emperor, Lord Morning Star, and most of the demon lords wear cloaks. Use the royal color of turquoise blue for the Emperor's design.

Materials
• plain paper
• markers
• 1 1/2 yards white cloth for each
• fabric or tempera paints
• paintbrushes

To Make
1. Draw your designs for the cloak on plain paper. You may want to use the patterns below.
2. Paint the design on the white cloth.
3. Allow to dry.

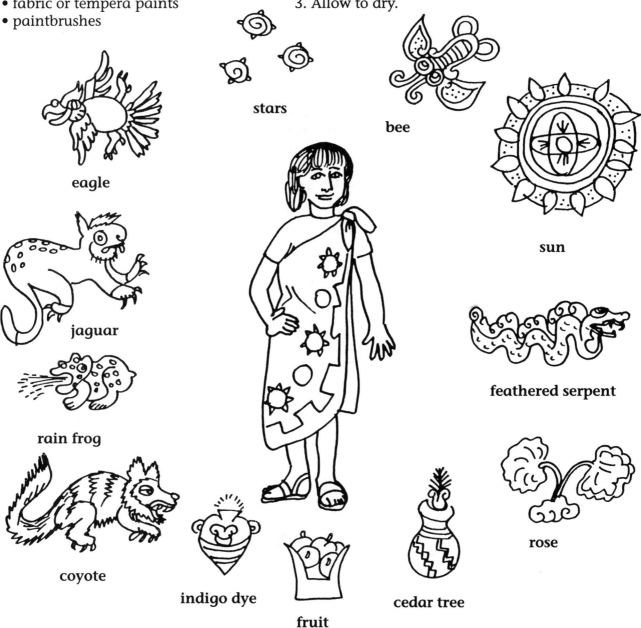

stars

bee

eagle

sun

jaguar

rain frog

feathered serpent

coyote

indigo dye

cedar tree

rose

fruit

To Wear: Pin or tie two corners over one shoulder as shown.

Jewelry

The ancient Aztecs were very fond of jewelry. Those who could afford them wore gold or silver ear plugs. Large necklaces were decorated with turquoise, other gems, or exotic bird feathers. Follow the directions below to make your own.

Ear Plugs

Materials
- cardboard or oak tag
- scissors
- gold or silver foil
- tape or glue
- dull pencil

To Make
1. Trace the ear plug pattern twice onto cardboard.
2. Cut out both ear plugs.
3. Cover the cardboard with foil. Tape or glue on the back of each ear plug.
4. To decorate, use a pencil to carefully draw Aztec designs on the foil.

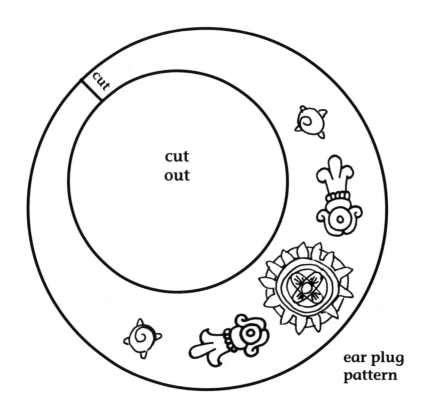

ear plug pattern

To Wear: Hook over the top of the ears.

Necklace

In the play most of the actors wear necklaces. Follow the directions below to make a basic necklace. Use colored paper, feathers, fake jewels, or dyed pasta shapes to decorate it and make it unique. Look at the art in the book to get Aztec design ideas.

Materials
- 11" x 17" oak tag
- 13" piece of string
- ruler
- pencil
- scissors
- hole punch
- 2–8" pieces of yarn
- glue
- decorations

To Make
1. Using a ruler and pencil, make tiny marks on the long side of the oak tag. Starting from one end, one mark should be made at 8 1/2", another at 5 1/2".
2. Tie the string close to the pointed end of the pencil.
3. Hold the end of the string at the center (8 1/2") pencil mark. Place the point of the pencil at the corner of the paper. While holding the string at the center mark, draw a semi circle with the pencil.
4. Repeat number 3 with the pencil at the 5 1/2" mark.
5. Cut out the necklace on the pencil lines.
6. Punch holes at the edge of the necklace as shown.
7. String holes with two pieces of yarn.
8. Decorate the necklace with Aztec designs.

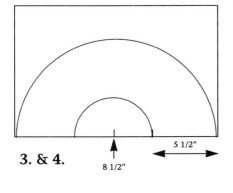

3. & 4.

8 1/2" 5 1/2"

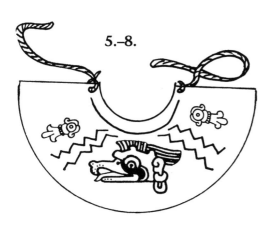

5.–8.

To Wear: Tie the yarn pieces behind the neck.

Arm or Leg Band

In the play most of the actors wear necklaces. Follow the directions below to make a basic necklace. Use colored paper, feathers, fake jewels, or dyed pasta shapes to decorate it and make it look unique. Look at the art in *The Flame of Peace* to get ideas.

Materials
- pattern at right copied on oak tag
- scissors
- hole punch
- heavy cord
- tacky glue
- gold paint

To Make
Partners take turns working with the glue and string.
1. Cut out arm band and punch holes on the tiny circles.
2. Cut cord into 12" lengths.
3. Put a thin line of glue along the center lines of the black design.
4. Put the cord along the glue line.
5. Continue gluing cord down over the design from the center to the outside.
6. Allow to dry.
7. Paint the whole band with gold paint. Allow to dry.
8. Tie 6" lengths of cord through each hole at the corners of the band.

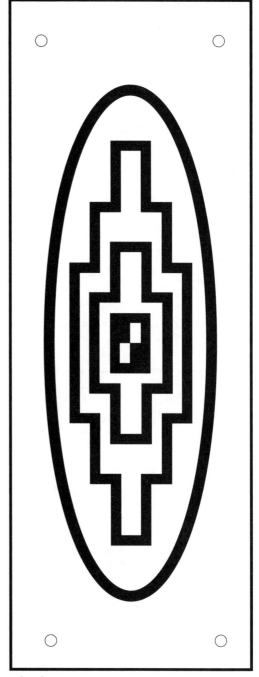

To Wear: Tie around upper arm or around leg just below the knee.

Headdresses

Aztec emperors and warriors wore elaborate headdresses made of feathers, jewels, or animal

Emperor's Headdress

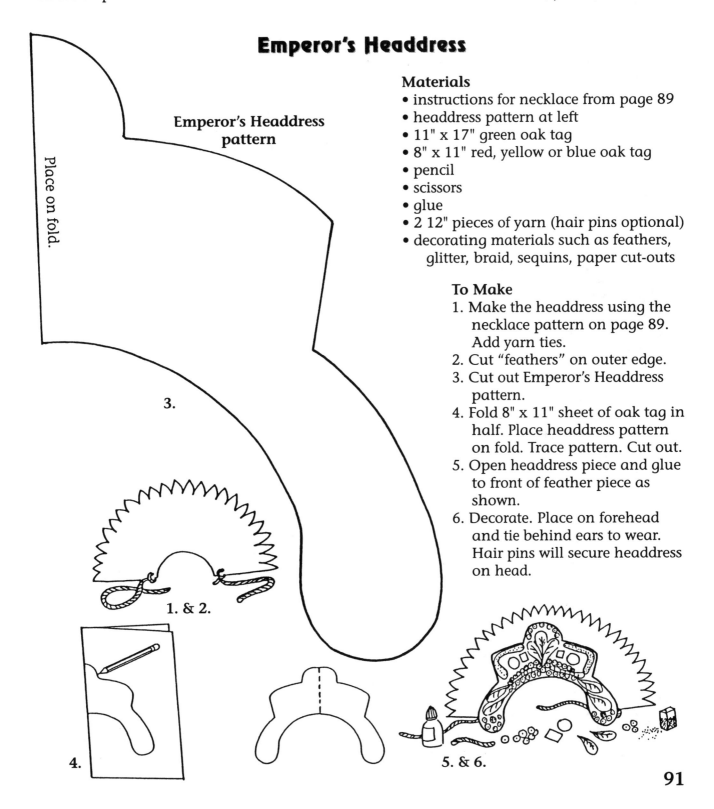

Emperor's Headdress
pattern

Place on fold.

3.

1. & 2.

4.

5. & 6.

Materials
- instructions for necklace from page 89
- headdress pattern at left
- 11" x 17" green oak tag
- 8" x 11" red, yellow or blue oak tag
- pencil
- scissors
- glue
- 2 12" pieces of yarn (hair pins optional)
- decorating materials such as feathers, glitter, braid, sequins, paper cut-outs

To Make
1. Make the headdress using the necklace pattern on page 89. Add yarn ties.
2. Cut "feathers" on outer edge.
3. Cut out Emperor's Headdress pattern.
4. Fold 8" x 11" sheet of oak tag in half. Place headdress pattern on fold. Trace pattern. Cut out.
5. Open headdress piece and glue to front of feather piece as shown.
6. Decorate. Place on forehead and tie behind ears to wear. Hair pins will secure headdress on head.

Warrior Headdress

Materials
- feather and glyph patterns below
- 24" piece of wide elastic per group
- red, blue, yellow (or gold) paper
- tacky glue
- scissors
- crayons, markers (optional)

To Make
1. Reproduce 2 sets of feather patterns per headdress on red and blue paper. Cut them out.
2. Reproduce 1 set of glyph patterns on yellow paper per headdress. Cut them out.
   Note: Crayons or markers can be used to add more color to the glyphs and feathers.
3. Lay the elastic flat on the table. Glue the leaves to the back of the elastic, alternating colors. Space evenly. Allow to set.
4. Glue the glyphs to the front of the elastic.
5. To wear, tie ends of elastic at the back of head.

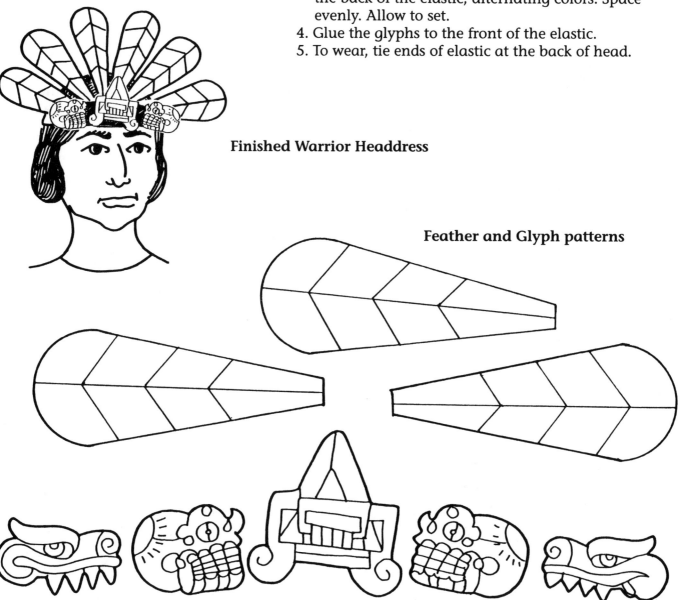

Finished Warrior Headdress

Feather and Glyph patterns

Weapons for Warriors

Shields

Warriors used shields to protect themselves in battle. Partners decorate a shield with one of the designs below or create another geometric or animal design.

Materials
- large pizza round or cardboard circle
- pencil
- markers or paints
- 3" x 10" piece of oak tag
- wide masking tape

To Make
1. Draw a design on the pizza round, using one of the designs shown or one of your own.
2. Color in the design with markers or paints. Allow to dry.
3. Tape the ends of the piece of oak tag to the center of the back, making a handle large enough to slip an arm through as shown below.

3.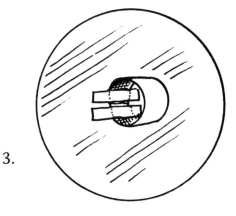

To Use: Slip arm through the handle and hold in front of body.

93

Spear

Aztec warriors used spears in battle, for hunting, for games, and during war dances. Points were made of obsidian. Make spears for the warriors to use in the play.

Materials
- 4 large sheets of newspaper
- masking tape
- 3 1/2" x 6" piece heavy cardboard
- scissors
- brown and grey paints
- paintbrush
- 3–24" pieces of wide gift ribbon

To Make
1. Tape two sheets of newspaper together overlapping the top and bottom to make a larger sheet. Repeat with other two sheets.
2. Stack the large sheets together.
3. Starting at one corner, roll the sheets together *very tightly* making a long stick. Tape securely.
4. Trace the spear point on heavy cardboard. Cut it out.
5. Tape the point to the stick.
6. Paint the stick brown and the spear point grey.
7. Decorate the spear by tying ribbons to the stick just below the point.

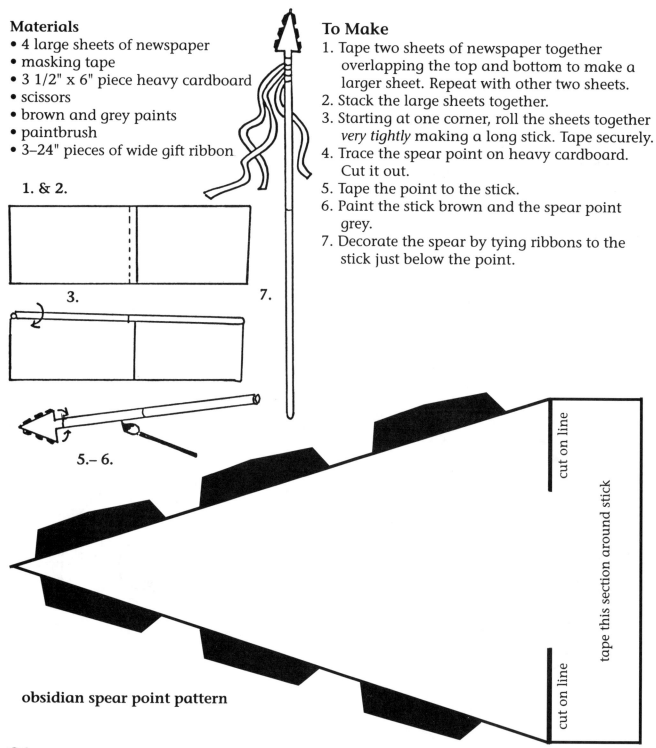

1. & 2.

3.

5.– 6.

7.

obsidian spear point pattern

cut on line

cut on line

tape this section around stick

94

The Flame of Peace

In the story Two Flint returns from the Hill of the Star with a feathery torch called the New Fire. He brought it back to the city, placed it on the altar in the temple, and brought peace to the Aztecs. Make a simular torch for the finale of the play. Or, use an orange or red feather duster decorated with glitter instead.

Materials
- cardboard paper towel core
- paper dessert cup
- artist knife
- masking tape
- gold or red paint
- red and gold tissue paper or cellophane
- orange, red, and yellow oak tag (for flames)
- glitter
- glue

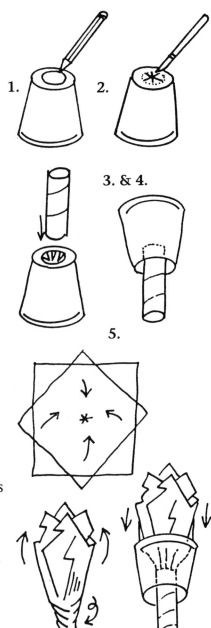

To Make
1. Trace the diameter of the paper towel core on the center of the bottom of the dessert cup.
2. Use an artist knife to carefully cut diagonal slashes across the circle on the bottom of the cup.
3. Push the towel core up through the hole in the cup so that it reaches just above the top of the cup. Tape to secure.
4. Paint the outside of the cup and paper towel core red or gold, whichever you prefer. Allow to dry.
5. Lay the red and gold tissue flat as shown. Grasp at center and pull outer edges inward and up, making tissue into "flames." Insert and glue the flames inside the paper cup.
6. Using the patterns on the following page, cut several flames of each size using orange, red, and yellow oak tag.
7. Dip the edges of the oak tag flames in glue and sprinkle with glitter. Allow to dry thoroughly.
8. Glue the flames to the top of the torch, overlapping around the towel core and the cup as shown. Allow to dry.

To Use: Lord Morning Star hands the torch to Two Flint, who carries it back to the temple altar. A clear plastic vase could be used to stand the torch on the altar.

Flame Patterns for the Torch

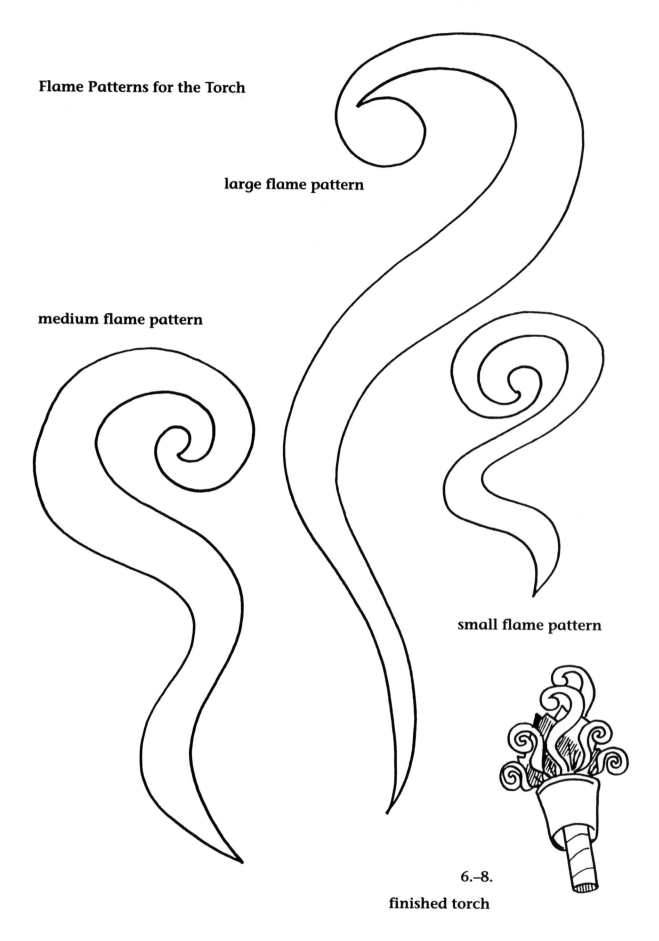

large flame pattern

medium flame pattern

small flame pattern

6.–8.

finished torch

Appendix
AN OVERVIEW OF COOPERATIVE LEARNING

What makes cooperative learning unique?

In a cooperative classroom, group activities are more than just children working together. Learning structures (called recipes here) guide children to respond to and interact with each other in specific ways. Every task has both an academic and social goal, which are evaluated at the end of the activity with self-monitoring as well as teacher observation.

Instead of competition, students working together learn positive interdependence, that they sink or swim together. Each student contributes their part to each activity or assignment. Each team gets a single grade based on all the members doing their part. Instead of a few top students being the stars, all members must learn and use the information for the group to be successful. Students even take on the role of instructor, presenting new material or helping teammates practice skills.

The benefits of cooperative learning:

In a cooperative classroom, you become a facilitator to learning, not the prime source of instruction. Students begin to see their classmates as important and valuable sources of knowledge. Essential interpersonal social skills learned step by step and reinforced in every lesson make the classroom climate more positive, more nurturing, as students learn to give each other encouragement and praise.

Students even benefit academically, because in a cooperative atmosphere they have more chances to understand the material through oral rehearsal, thinking out loud, and discussing their views with others. Children learn that their differences make for a stronger team.

CLASSROOM GUIDELINES
GROUPING AND SOCIAL SKILLS

Planning for grouping and social skills:

Lessons have been planned for you so that the academic and social skills are built into the activity. This way, even if you have not worked with cooperative learning before, you can organize your groups quickly, spending your time monitoring and evaluating social progress.

Team groupings will be suggested for the activities. Primary classrooms work best in pairs because it is easier for children to decide or agree with one other person. Once they are working well in pairs, advance to threes and then two sets of pairs to make four. Unless your project demands it (such as a culminating activity having four or six distinct parts), four is the suggested upper limit for groups.

When choosing pairs, you may want to choose randomly or assign pairs to mix abilities and temperaments. Occasionally, you will find an "oil-and-water" pair, or a child who has trouble working with any partner and needs to be changed frequently. Once you have groups of four, make sure they are heterogeneous and have ample opportunity to "gel" as a group and learn to work together. Resist the temptation to break up groups who are having problems. Emphasize the social skills they need to learn and practice to get them all working together.

Defining and developing social skills:

Many teachers shy away from a group approach because they think of all the problems associated with groups of children working together: confusion, noise, personality conflicts, differences of opinion, etc. Cooperative teaching does not assume children have the social skills needed to work together successfully. The behaviors that enhance group progress are introduced, explained, modeled, practiced, and evaluated like any other skill.

To use cooperative learning successfully, it is important for you to be aware of the social skills appropriate for each activity. Introduce them at the beginning of each lesson, define, reinforce, and evaluate them at the completion of the assignment. As you groups develop, you may want to emphasize and build on other social skills of your choice. With older groups (grades 4–5), co-op activities are the ideal vehicle to experiment with learning and problem-solving skills. You can introduce these along with the simpler social skills.

These are the Interpersonal Group skills necessary in grades 1–5:

COMING TOGETHER (grades 1–5)
- form groups quietly
- stay in the group
- discuss quietly
- participate
- use names, make eye contact
- speak clearly
- listen actively
- allow no put-downs

WORKING TOGETHER (grades 1–5)
- work toward goal, purpose, time limit
- praise others, seek others' ideas
- ask for help when needed
- paraphrase other members' contributions
- energize group
- describe one's feelings when appropriate

LEARNING TOGETHER (grades 3–5)
- summarize material
- seek accuracy by correcting, giving information
- elaborate
- jog memory of teammates
- explain reasons for answers/beliefs
- plan aloud to teach concepts, agree on approaches

PROBLEM-SOLVING SKILLS (grades 4–5)
- criticize ideas, not people
- differentiate where there is disagreement
- integrate a number of ideas into a single conclusion
- ask for justification
- extend another's answer by adding to it
- probe by asking questions
- generate further answers
- check answers/conclusions with original instruction

Teaching social skills:

- Work on one social skill at a time. Add others slowly as groups are ready.
- Introduce the skill and discuss why it is important.
- Define in words and actions what children will see and hear as they are using that skill in their groups. Look through the materials in the classroom management sections to find charts, hand-outs, and other materials to help to do this.
- Give a demonstration for the children to follow (modeling).
- Set up practice situations and refer to the charts, etc., as children practice the skill.
- Praise lavishly attempts to use a skill, repeat words/deeds done showing it.
- At the end of the session, give children time to think whether they used the skill in the session or not. Evaluate them by the use of the teacher charts provided or have them vote as a group as to whether they think they succeeded and why.
- Be patient with yourself and the students. Social skills need to be practiced often to become natural.

98

COOPERATIVE GUIDELINES: PREPARING LESSONS

Along with the team grouping suggestions, cooperative recipes for learning (sometimes called practice structures) are used with the activities in this book. The symbol for the recipe is clearly shown on each lesson. The academic and social skills to be emphasized are beside each symbol. This will help you to organize the class and choose the lessons you wish to use.

The recipes provided each reinforce a number of social skills and guide children to process information in their groups in a variety of ways. For the first time through the materials, we suggest you use the recipe with one or two of the social skills listed near the symbols for each activity. However, when you are familiar with the projects, you can emphasize other skills. It is our hope that you will make the lessons your own, adapting them to your particular classroom. As you work through each, they will become natural to you and your students. They will make a positive impact on your classroom atmosphere and student performance. The key is to be patient and give children time to learn and practice each recipe.

COOPERATIVE CLASSROOM RECIPES

 ## Sharing Circle

Social skills: Listen actively, participate, clear speech

Group size: Whole class

Directions: Children sit in a large circle, so each student can see the rest. The leader (teacher or student) starts an open-ended statement or sentence, and each student in turn ends it with their own statement. If they can't think of an answer at that time, they can pass, but are expected to have their answer ready by the time the circle is completed.

 ## Round Robin

Social skills: Vocalization, time limit, quick associations, participate, extend another's answers, building team spirit

Group size: 3–4

Directions: This is an oral counterpart to Roundtable. **Note:** This is an excellent method for brainstorming vocabulary, problem solving, or creating an oral story together. It is also excellent for younger students with limited writing skills.

 ## Roundtable

Social skills: Time limit, quick associations, participate, extend another's answers

Group size: 3–4

Directions: All team members contribute ideas to one sheet of paper. Make sure the team members know the direction the paper should be passed. When the signal is given, members write or draw the answer and pass it on.

 ## Simultaneous Roundtable

Social skills: Time limit, waiting politely, discussing quietly, participating

Group size: 3–4

Directions: More than one sheet is passed within the group. Members start with one sheet each and pass it on.

Study Group

Social skills: Paraphrasing, positive support, time limit, group purpose

Group size: 2–4

Directions: Present information in a traditional way. Children get into their small groups to complete a cooperative assignment that reinforces, expands on, or tests their knowledge. Groups can brainstorm, fill out a K W L chart within their groups to set goals for further study or complete various activities like word webbing. **Note:** Use the role cards and discussion strips to help keep social skills moving while in groups. Another quick associations recipe is **Numbered Heads Together.**

Numbered Heads Together

Social skills: Use quiet voices, participate, time limit, quick associations, elaborate, integration, team energizing, and praise

Group Size: 2–4

Note: For this activity, you will need a code or signal to get all groups attention: lights on/off, a bell, or hand signal. Use it with other recipes as needed.

Directions: Students are in groups, listening to instruction by teacher. When a question is posed, the teacher tells the groups to put their heads together and discuss it. This gives students a chance to immediately discuss the information and figure out the right response together. After a time is given for discussion, the teacher signals for attention. At this time, students number off within each group. The teacher calls one number, and a representative from each group gives the team's answer. Team points are given for correct responses. **Note:** For simultaneous responses, team can members write a response on the chalkboard.

Interview

Social skills: Using names, eye contact, paraphrasing, summarizing, describing feelings, probing for answers, vocalization

Group size: 3–4

Note: This format is good to prepare for a unit or to close a unit.

Directions: Members take turns interviewing each other. After they have all had a chance to share, have the group round-robin (described at right) what they learned from the interviews. For example, each child could take on one of the characters from an event or story and give his or her perspective. Use of role cards or discussion strips, so each asks a pertinent question, will help it go smoothly.

Team Share

Social skills: Planning to teach, elaborate, vocalization, ways to jog memory, extend another's answers, integrate a number of ideas

Group size: 3–4

Note: This is an ideal way to have teams share products or projects with each other. Be sure to give teams time to plan how they will present themselves.

Directions: When teams have completed various projects, have them get ready to share with other teams. Organize the class so each team is clearly marked and knows where they are to go. For instance, a blue #1 card goes to one team, a blue #2 card goes to another, and they meet at the blue station. Team #1 shares first, team #2 is the audience. Then they switch. If you have an uneven number of teams, you can pair up with one or put three groups together.

Co-op Cards

Social skills: Using names, eye contact, positive statements, jog memory

Group size: Do first with partners, then in groups of 4.

Note: This format is an invaluable method for memory work and drill; children learn while praising each other and supporting each other's efforts.

Directions: Give each pair or study group a set of the Co-op Cards you want them to learn. Then, they learn to play these games:

Game 1: Maximum Help
Partner 1 hands his card to partner 2. Partner 2, the teacher, shows the cards and the answers one by one, to Partner 1, the student, who repeats the words or answers. Cards done correctly are won back with lots of praise from the teacher. Cards done incorrectly are repeated and explained thoroughly by the tutor and asked again. When all cards are won back, they switch roles.

Game 2: Minimum Help
Partner 1 hands his card to partner 2. Partner 2, the teacher, shows the cards one by one to partner 1, the student, who answers. Cards done correctly are won back with lots of praise from the teacher. Cards done incorrectly are repeated with some hints. When all cards are won back, they switch roles.

Game 3: No Help
Partner 1 hands his card to partner 2. Partner 2, the teacher, shows the cards one by one to partner 1, the student, who answers. Cards done correctly are won back with lots of praise from the teacher. Cards done incorrectly are put back into the teacher's stack to be repeated with no hints. When all cards are won back, they switch roles.

Evaluation: Groups can keep a chart showing all words learned, with an envelope for those words that still need to be practiced and won.

Note: To keep the game fresh, the teacher should continually think of new and grander praises.

 ## Turn to Your Partner

Social skills: Using names, eye contact, listen actively, quiet voices, paraphrasing

Group size: 2

Directions: As you present material, have students pair up to share ideas, information, or opinions. This works best when you use established partners who sit near each other already, in order to minimize the amount of class time spent on moving toward partners. It is a good way to quickly reinforce active listening and early social skills.

 ## Pairs Check or Partners

Social skills: Accuracy, energizing, positive support, ways to jog memory

Group size: 2

Directions: Teams work in pairs. In each pair, one player does a problem. The other is the coach in every sense of the word, giving help, praise, and encouragement! Switch roles after every problem. When two problems are completed, pairs must check with each other and agree on the answers. This is a good time to have a team handshake. Then proceed to the next two problems in the same way. Remember to keep your pairs heterogeneous for activities like this, so there is a range of abilities to keep things moving.

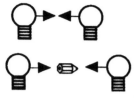

Think, Pair, Share, Think, Write, Pair, Share

Social skills: Paraphrasing, memory of content, vocalization

Group size: 2

Directions: Similar to Turn to Your Partner, but when more time is wanted on task. Present material, have students pair up to think about the content just presented, share ideas, information or opinions. This works well when you use established partners, but can also be used to exchange pairs to get different opinions. If you have children write down their idea (and it is a good idea, so they won't be swayed or lose direction), you can pair them up with others who think the same thing or have different opinions. **Note:** For another way to group by opinion or interest, see **Pick Your Spot.**

Pick Your Spot (Corners)

Social skills: Vocalization, groups by interest or opinion

Group size: 4–6
Note: By having children write down responses ahead of time, they will stay on task better and get to their places quicker. You can see where they're headed and direct them to the right corner.
Directions: Pose a question or topic with four answers or subtopics and have each child select which of the four would be their choice. Have them write it down and go to the corner of the room where that topic or answer is displayed. This is a quick way to get children with similar interests together to do further study, share opinions, or become roving reporters to teach the rest of the class.
Note: For another way to group children by interest or opinion see **Line-Ups.**

Line-Ups

Social skills: Vocalization, probing for information, sharing reasons for answer

Group size: Whole class or split in half for two lines

Note: This works best in probing an answer or problem with a range of opinions.

Directions: Create a masking tape line on your classroom floor divided into three categories; yes/ maybe/no, always/ sometimes/never, etc. Pose a question or situation. Children write down their answer on small slips of paper. Then, they line up on the line that nearest matches their opinion. Once they're on the line, they can use the information discussing with their immediate group their reasons for choosing that answer or leave their paper markers in place and go back to their desks to look and compare how many are in each section and make a class opinion graph. Some classroom teachers have developed lively discussions by having the children pair with members from other sections to discuss why they had different opinions. The tape line can remain in place to be used later.

Stand and Share

Social skills: Speak clearly, listen actively, participate, time limit

Group size: 2–4

Directions: As in Study Group, teams ready themselves on a specific topic. Teams or members within each team number off. When the teacher calls a number, all the team members must stand and be ready to answer the question. As you call the numbers, that team or member answers the questions and sits down. This is good for an oral quiz or checking problems where all members need to know the information.

CLASSROOM MANAGEMENT CHARTS AND BUTTONS

These materials will help you define, display, and reinforce social lessons.

Social Skills T-Chart

To use: Enlarge and reproduce full-page or poster-size. Write the social skill to be learned in the top section as you discuss its importance. Have your classes brainstorm how it looks when children are using that skill, as well as how it sounds when it's happening. This gives the children a solid basis for modeling and monitoring their social behavior. Display it prominently and refer to it often. Laminate and save. Use the chart whenever that skill is being emphasized.

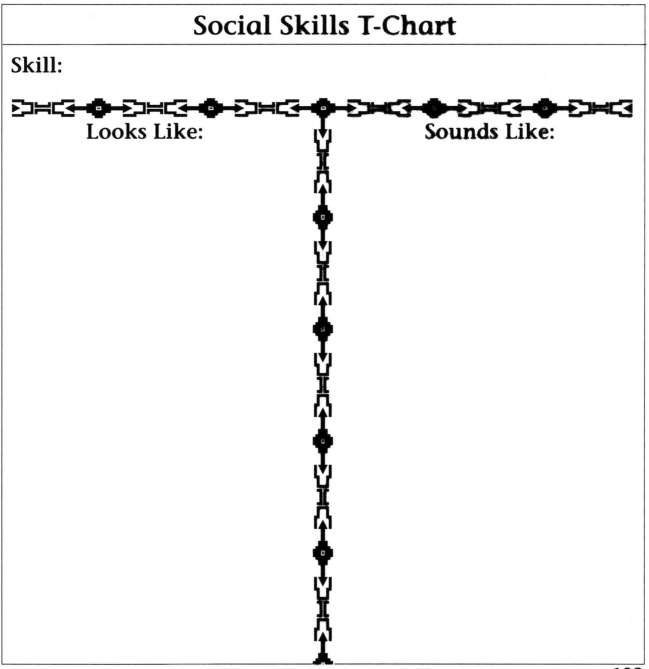

Social Skills T-Chart

Skill:

Looks Like: **Sounds Like:**

PRAISE WORDS

To use: In order to increase the kind and frequency of encouraging words in the classroom, brainstorm suggestions and write them in open areas within the design. Keep them on display. As you hear others, add them to the chart with plenty of praises of your own.

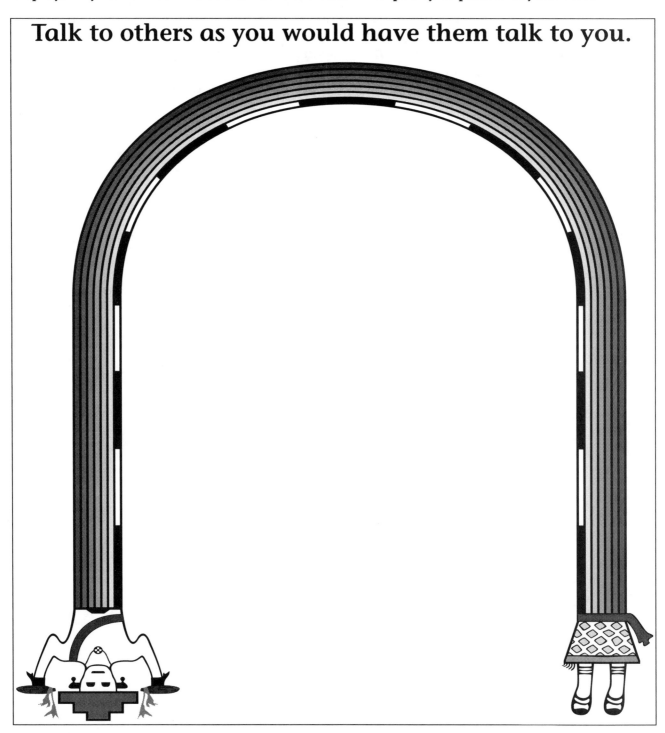

Talk to others as you would have them talk to you.

Note: For a class with ingrained negative habits, it may also be helpful to put up a list of TABOO or OFF-LIMITS sayings. These can be placed on another chart with a line through them or the title "COOPERATIVE NO-NOs!"

DISCUSSION STRIPS

To use: Reproduce the strips you will use on as many different colors of paper as there are members of each team. Each student gets appropriate strips to use during group discussions. Whenever a student contributes, a strip is "spent." Discussion goes on until all have used their strips. This keeps all members contributing equally, and aware of *how* they are responding.
Note: Younger groups may need practice in many of these modes before it comes naturally to them, so start simply. Children can bring in envelopes to store the strips in for later use.

	Answer a Question		Ask a Question
	Check for Understanding		Encourage Your Group
	Give a Praise Word		Share an Idea
	Keep Your Group on Task		Paraphrase
	Respond to an Idea		Summarize Progress

EVALUATION TOOLS

TEACHER OBSERVATION FORM

To use: When your groups are working, use this form as you circulate, observe, and record their progress. Be sure to write quotes and repeat them to reinforce and model behavior during and after the activity.

Teacher Observation Chart

Skill: _____

GROUP	STUDENTS	COMMENTS

K-W-L CHART

To use: Children discuss an upcoming topic and fill in questions for the K, W, and L sections. Reproduce full-page size for use in small groups to focus learning or poster-size as a whole-class exercise to introduce a topic.

K= What I KNOW about: _____.
W= WHAT I would like to find out: _____.
L= What I have LEARNED: _____.

ROLE BUTTONS

To use: Reproduce on sturdy oaktag and cut out. When children are doing group work, the badges will remind each of their group job. Use only the buttons that are applicable to the activity. You will also find it easier to check if students are performing as they should because you can see at a glance what each member's role is within the group.

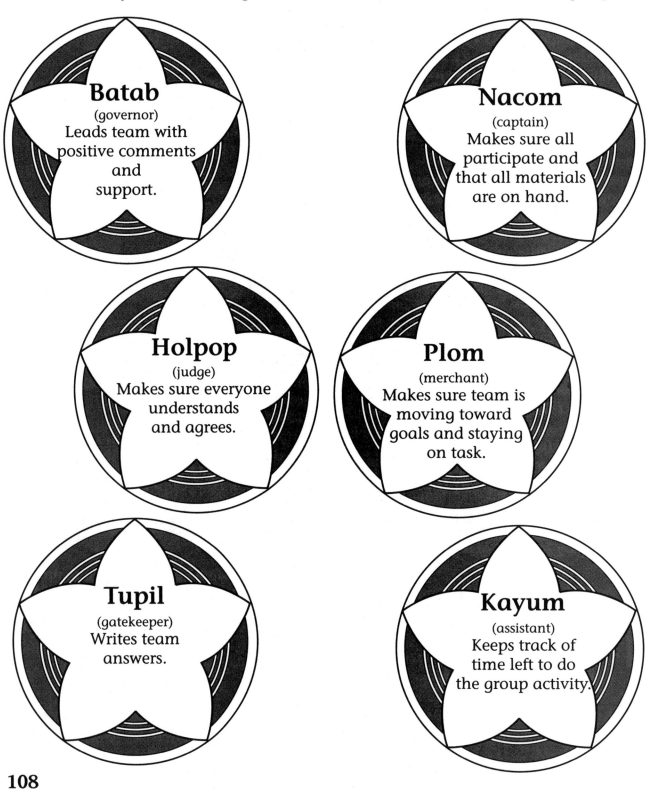

Batab
(governor)
Leads team with positive comments and support.

Nacom
(captain)
Makes sure all participate and that all materials are on hand.

Holpop
(judge)
Makes sure everyone understands and agrees.

Plom
(merchant)
Makes sure team is moving toward goals and staying on task.

Tupil
(gatekeeper)
Writes team answers.

Kayum
(assistant)
Keeps track of time left to do the group activity.

GROUP EVALUATION FORM

To use: Take a few minutes after an activity for teams to evaluate their progress. The group form should be agreed upon by members, filled in, and initialed by all. The form will be helpful when groups are having problems and be able to spot areas needing improvement.

How Are We Doing?

Group: _____ Date: _____

Because: *Initial:*

1. We marched ahead: _____   _____

2. We reached our goal: _____   _____

3. We lost our way: _____   _____

4. We lost the battle: _____   _____

5. We had a smooth journey: _____   _____

AWARD CERTIFICATE

To use: When you see groups accomplishing goals, give them a visual reminder of their progress. Groups can earn them, barter them, display them with team pride, or use toward whole-class goals.

Paying Tribute to

_____

for helping us conquer our goals and making this class successful in creating and learning!

signed: _____

date: _____

Bibliography

Many materials were used in preparation of this book. The following list should be used as a starting point. Your local librarian can help you find other appropriate materials.

Aztec, Inca & Maya by by Elizabeth Baquedano (Alfred A. Knopf, 1993)

Aztecs and Spaniards: Cortes and the Conquest of Mexico by Albert Marin (Atheneum, 1986)

Aztecs by Frances F. Berdan (Chelsea House Publishers, 1989)

The Aztecs by Judith Crosloer (Silver, 1985)

The Aztecs by Pamela Odijk (Silver Burdett, 1989)

Aztecs revised edition by Jill Hughes (Glousecter, 1987)

The Aztecs revised edition by Penny Bateman (Franklin Watts, 1988)

Aztecs, a Civilization Project Book by Susan Purdy and Cass R. Sandak, (Franklin Watts, 1982)

The Aztecs, The Ancient World by Pamela Odijk (Silver Burdett Press, 1989)

Aztecs: Facts, Things to Make Activities by Ruth Thomson (Franklin Watts, 1992)

Aztecs: See Through History by Tim Wood (Viking Press, 1992)

The Expeditions of Cortes by Nigel Hunter (Bookwright, 1990)

A Family in Peru by Jetty St. John (Lerner Publications Company, 1987)

The Flame of Peace, a Tale of the Aztecs by Doborah Nourse Lattimore (Harper & Row, 1987)

Growing up in Aztec Times by Brenda R. Lewis (Batsford, 1981)

How They Lived, An Aztec Warrior by Anne Steel (Rourke Enterprises, Inc., 1988)

How They Lived, An Inca Farmer by Marion Morrison (Rourke Enterprises, Inc., 1986)

The Incas by Anne Millard (Warwick Press, 1980)

The Incas Knew by Tilie S. Pine and Joseph Levine (McGraw-Hill, 1968)

The Incas, a New True Book by Pat McKissack (Children's Press, 1985)

Indians of Mexico by Margaret C. Farquhar (Holt, Rinehart and Winston, 1967)

Lost in the Clouds, the Discovery of Machu Picchu by Elizabeth Gemming (Coward, McCann and Geohegan, Inc. 1980)

The Maya by Green (Franklin Watts, 1992)

Maya by Pat MiKissack (Children's Press, 1985)

Maya by Trout (Chelsea House, 1991)

The Maya Knew by Tillie S. Pine and Joseph Levine (McGraw Hill, 1971)

Maya, Land of the Turkey and the Deer by Victor W. von Hagen (The World Publishing Company, 1960)

Maya: A Simulation of Mayan Civilization During the Seventh Century by Peter Roth (Interaction Publishers, 1993)

*Maya*s by Pamela Odijk (Silver Burdett, 1990)

The Night of the Scorpion by Anthon Horowitz (Pacer Books, 1984)

Pizarro and the Conquest of Peru by Cecil Howard (American Heritage Publishing Co., Inc., 1968)

Pyramid of the Sun, Pyramid of the Moon by Leonard Everett Fisher (Macmillan, 1988)

Rand McNally Children's Atlas of North Americans: Native Cultures of North and South America by Francis Reddy (Rand McNally, 1992)

See Inside an Aztec Town, edited by R. J. Unstead (Warwick Press, 1980)

The Spread of Civilization by Ron Carter (Silver Burdett, 1979)

This Place Is High by Vicki Cobb (Walker and Company, 1989)

Cooperative Learning References

Circles of Learning, Cooperation in the Classroom by David W. Johnson, Roger T. Johnson, Edythe Johnson Holubec, Patricia Roy (Association for Supervision and Curriculum Development, 1984)

Cooperative Learning: Getting Started by Susan Ellis and Susan Whalen (Scholastic, Inc., 1990)

Cooperative Learning Lessons for Little Ones by Lorna Curan (Resource for Teachers, 1990)

Index